P9-BZB-637

'2/25/22

"LKY"

# THE
# BIG
# IDEAS
## OF
## LEE KUAN YEW

d. 92
d. 2015
b. 1923

Published by Straits Times Press Pte Ltd
Singapore Press Holdings
Mezzanine Floor, Information Resource Centre
Level 3, Podium Block
1000 Toa Payoh North, News Centre
Singapore 318994
Tel: (65) 6319 6319 Fax: (65) 6319 8258
stpressbooks@sph.com.sg
www.stpressbooks.com.sg

STRAITS TIMES PRESS
Executive Director, Shirley Hew
Publishing Manager, Shova Loh
Creative Director, Lock Hong Liang
Marketing & Operations, Clara Wong
Editor, Mary Lee

© 2015 Lee Kuan Yew School of Public Policy
& Straits Times Press

All rights reserved. No part of this publication may be reproduced,
stored in a retrieval system, or transmitted, in any form or by any
means, electronic, mechanical, photocopying, recording or otherwise,
without the prior written permission of the copyright owners.

Printed in Singapore

**National Library Board, Singapore
Cataloguing-in-Publication Data**

The big ideas of Lee Kuan Yew / edited by Shashi Jayakumar and
Rahul Sagar. – Singapore : Straits Times Press, 2014
pages cm
Includes index.
ISBN : 978-981-4342-79-7 (hardcover)

1. Political planning – Singapore. 2. Singapore – Politics and
government – 1965-1990. 3. Lee, Kuan Yew, 1923-  I. Jayakumar,
Shashi, editor. II. Sagar, Rahul, editor.
JQ1063.A56
320.95957 — dc23     OCN890638505

THE
# BIG
# IDEAS
OF
## LEE KUAN YEW

EDITED BY

SHASHI JAYAKUMAR

AND

RAHUL SAGAR

Straits Times Press

# CONTENTS

# INTRODUCTION

# Lee Kuan Yew's Complex Legacy

*Kishore Mahbubani*

# LEE KUAN YEW'S COMPLEX LEGACY

*Kishore Mahbubani*

WHEN THE DUST has settled and the histories of the 20th century are written and lists are produced of the ten greatest men of the century, there is no doubt that one name from Singapore will feature on many of the lists: Lee Kuan Yew. Many know that he was the key man behind the successful transformation of Singapore. Few know the larger geographical footprint of his impact. When the major archives are opened and the notes of conversations between Mr Lee and the great world leaders of the 20th century are declassified and released, they will show that Lee Kuan Yew influenced many key minds and influenced them significantly. In so doing, he shifted the course of world history from time to time.

Richard Nixon, one of the great leaders of the 20th century, once lamented: "The fact that a leader of Mr Lee's breadth of vision was not able to act on a broader stage represents an incalculable loss to the world." Yet, paradoxically, Richard Nixon never failed to give credit to Mr Lee for influencing his global perspectives. Similarly, President Nixon's legendary secretary of state, Henry Kissinger, never hesitated to endorse Mr Lee as one of the greatest leaders of his time. "There is no better strategic thinker in the world today. Two generations of American leaders have benefited from his counsel," Secretary Kissinger wrote in *Time* magazine.

This is why this book is important. It is the very first attempt by a group of policymakers and scholars that have worked for and with Lee Kuan Yew to reflect on his contributions. Fortunately, Mr Lee himself has produced several volumes which have tried to document all his contributions and his views. Yet, as Mr Lee has been careful not to praise himself, he has been somewhat modest about his contributions to world history. Our School hopes this book will be the first of many to assess Lee Kuan Yew's legacy.

His legacy will be complex. And it will be complex because Mr Lee is a complex man. He stands out in at least five ways. First, he is a deeply thoughtful man. In comparison with his Southeast Asian peers (with whom he collaborated to found, after the EU, the second most successful regional organisation in the world, namely ASEAN), he stood out as a towering intellectual. Neither Tunku Abdul Rahman of Malaysia nor President Suharto of Indonesia could match the quality of his mind. Nor could President Ferdinand Marcos of the Philippines or Prime Minister Thanom Kittikachorn of Thailand. It was no surprise, therefore, that Mr Lee was the only Southeast Asian leader to appear on *Foreign Policy*'s list of the top 100 public intellectuals in the world in 2008. This intellectual streak was reinforced by two great minds he worked with, namely Dr Goh Keng Swee and S Rajaratnam and, most importantly, by his brilliant wife, Kwa Geok Choo.

Second, unlike many thoughtful men, who sometimes suffer from paralysis through analysis, Mr Lee was a man of action. Though a great public intellectual in his own right, he displayed contempt towards individuals who were not prepared to combine good theory with good practice. One thing I learnt from working personally with Mr Lee was that he was an extremely

<u>results-oriented p</u>erson. When he failed to get the results he wanted from his instructions, he was known to have told a public official who failed him, "I don't accept excuses; I only recognise failures." Like his peers, Dr Goh Keng Swee and Howe Yoon Chong, he was a tough taskmaster. Yet there was no way that Singaporean society could have shed some of its negative traits of sloth and inertia without the kind of toughness that the first generation of Singapore's leaders displayed. This is why many Singaporean civil servants lived in fear then. Unlike their counterparts in many other countries who had security of tenure, Singaporean civil servants could be sacked, even senior civil servants who were found lacking.

<u>Third</u>, while Mr Lee was tough and determined, he was also <u>pragmatic</u>. If he discovered that he and his colleagues had charged up the wrong hill, he was prepared to reverse course and try different approaches. Hence, when a political explosion followed Howe Yoon Chong's effort to suddenly increase the age for withdrawing Central Provident Fund (CPF) savings in 1984, Mr Lee and his colleagues quietly and pragmatically reversed course. They were also prepared to learn lessons from all corners of the world. Dr Goh Keng Swee, who was probably Mr Lee's closest partner in government, used to say consistently that he had learnt a lot of lessons from the Meiji reformers of the 1860s. He stressed that they successfully transformed Japan because they learnt lessons from all over the world. Dr Goh once said to me: "<u>No matter what problem we encounter in Singapore, somebody somewhere in the world has successfully solved the problem. We should study their solutions and adapt them</u> intelligently to Singaporean society." Mr Lee was <u>equally</u> pragmatic.

<u>Fourth</u>, as pragmatism is sometimes associated in the West with an approach devoid of values and principles, it is vital to emphasise here that

Mr Lee was guided by some deeply held values. Corruption was a scourge in Singapore when he first took office in 1959. He and his colleagues were able to destroy this scourge because they led by example. They did not take a penny while they were in office. And they viewed with total contempt all the leaders in Asia who were filling their personal coffers while they were in office. Of course, there were several attempts to bribe high levels of the Singapore government. One of the most famous incidents took place in the early years, in 1961, when the CIA tried to bribe an officer in Singapore's Special Branch. Mr Lee was furious upon learning of this attempt and ordered that a trap be laid to catch the CIA officers red-handed. The CIA then attempted to bribe Mr Lee to cover up the incident, offering US$1 million not to Singapore but to the People's Action Party. The American government initially denied this but Mr Lee responded by releasing to the public a letter addressed to him by Secretary of State Dean Rusk apologising for the incident. Even so Mr Lee exhibited a sense of balance, cautioning the head of Singapore's Special Branch, Richard Corridon, to "remember all the time that we are not dealing with an enemy, but the bloody stupidity of a friend".

This incident with the CIA also demonstrated the fifth defining characteristic of Mr Lee: his courage. Several times in his career, Mr Lee demonstrated that he was prepared to fight greater opponents even when the odds were stacked against him. When he took on the communists, he knew that the odds were against him as they had developed a stronger control of the political ground in the 1950s. And when he forged a political coalition with them, he must have also known that all the politicians who had ridden the communist tiger at that time were eaten by it. Mr Lee turned out to be one of the few who rode this tiger and ate it up. Similarly, when he battled the Malay communalists in Malaysia he knew that they controlled all the guns. He could have been arrested by them or beaten by them (and as the 13 May 1969 riots showed, four years after Singapore left Malaysia, these Malay communalists were prepared to violently suppress Chinese dissenters). Yet Mr Lee never hesitated to fight if he believed that the cause was right.

This is why this book is valuable. It provides good illustrations of these defining characteristics of Lee Kuan Yew. It would be good to begin illustrating these points with the fifth characteristic – courage. SR Nathan's essay tells a remarkable story that illustrated Mr Lee's courage. In 1976, when Mr Lee was on his first official visit to China, he was presented by then Chinese Prime Minister Hua Guofeng with a copy of Neville Maxwell's *India's China War*, a pro-China history of the Sino-Indian War in 1962. Mr Lee handed the book back to him and said: "Mr Prime Minister, this is your version of the war. There is another version, the Indian version. And in any case I am from Southeast Asia – it's nothing to do with us."

Quite naturally, Mr Lee's reaction provoked an icy reaction from the Chinese delegation. In theory, an episode like this could have derailed relations between a great power and a small state like Singapore. In practice, the firm and clear stand taken by Mr Lee on behalf of Singapore actually raised the standing of Mr Lee and Singapore in the eyes of China's leaders. The Chinese leaders were probably aware of Vladimir Lenin's famous maxim: "Probe with a bayonet: if you meet steel, stop. If you meet mush, then push."

By demonstrating a steely spine in his dealings with great powers, Mr Lee helped to expand the geopolitical space for Singapore. The encounter with Hua Guofeng took place in 1976. Almost 20 years later, Singapore came under significant pressure from the president of the United States, Bill Clinton, not to cane an American teenager, Michael Fay, who had been

12

convicted of vandalism. Most countries expected Singapore to crumble under American pressure. I was the permanent secretary of the Singapore Foreign Ministry then. An ambassador from a relatively major country based in Singapore said to me: "Kishore, if a similar incident happened in my country, we would find a way of smuggling Michael Fay out of the country to avoid a confrontation with the sole superpower of the day." He was therefore truly shocked when the little country of Singapore stood firm and proceeded with the caning. The United States reacted angrily and froze several aspects of bilateral relations. That was a loss. However, the gains were much bigger as Singapore's firm stand against strong American pressure also helped to expand Singapore's geopolitical space in the region.

The episode with Michael Fay also demonstrated another aspect of Mr Lee's character: his firm commitment to certain principles, especially the rule of law. He firmly believed that no one should stand above the law in Singapore. Equally importantly, he believed that Singapore needed to develop strong judicial institutions and processes. This is why the essays of Prof S Jayakumar and former Chief Justice Chan Sek Keong are very important. Both played a very significant role in developing the institutions and processes in the field. And both worked closely with Mr Lee. Hence, they knew how committed he was to some fundamental principles of the rule of law.

There is no doubt that Mr Lee's training as a lawyer in the United Kingdom influenced his attitudes considerably. This is why Prof Jayakumar underscores that "his British education and exposure influenced his view of fair play which is why he retained judicial review, ensuring that public bodies with statutory powers behaved legally and fairly". Prof Jayakumar also addresses squarely the claim that has sometimes been made that the

Singapore government has used legal processes to further its political ends. He challenges the myth that Mr Lee was "confident that the judges will always rule in his favour". Many in Singapore have avoided discussion of such sensitive issues. It is good that Prof Jayakumar has challenged these myths.

Prof Jayakumar also addresses another important dimension of Mr Lee's views: his emphasis on order first and law second. In his early years, especially in the years of the Japanese occupation of Singapore and the years of fighting the communists, Mr Lee saw what happens to a society when order breaks down. This emphasis on establishing order first also comes out in the essay by Chan Sek Keong. In a very significant paragraph in his essay, he quotes Mr Lee as saying:

14

And when a state of increasing disorder and defiance of authority cannot be checked by the rules then existing, new and sometimes drastic rules have to be forged to maintain order so that the law can continue to govern human relations. The alternative is to surrender order for chaos and anarchy. So it is that we have to allow the use of extraordinary powers of detention, first in the case of political offenders under the [Preservation of Public Security Ordinance] and next in the case of secret society gangsters under the [Criminal Law (Temporary Provisions) Ordinance].

Chan also acknowledges that these practices in Singapore "do not measure well" against "the practices of individual liberty in two centuries of peaceful non-revolutionary England". This discussion highlights another instance when Mr Lee was prepared to defy conventional wisdom in the West if he felt that Singapore's unique circumstances demanded that a different approach be taken. One point that Chan does not make in his essay and which should be emphasised in this volume is that Mr Lee's tough approach was vindicated by the actions of the United States after 9/11. Despite the strong tradition of individual liberty in the United States, it did not hesitate to suspend "the ideas of habeas corpus and precedents of individual liberty" when it came face to face with the new threat of international terrorism. Indeed, the United States had earlier suspended its commitment to individual liberty when it interned Japanese Americans in various camps during World War II without any due process. As we move towards a complex global environment, it is clear that Mr Lee's views on order and law will be examined even more closely in coming years. This is another reason why this volume is truly timely.

Just as Mr Lee was both pragmatic and principled in his attitudes towards the issues of order and law, he was equally pragmatic and principled in his attitudes towards the issue of language in Singapore. For pragmatic reasons, he chose English as the working language of administration. This was a wise decision. It made Singapore internationally competitive. By contrast, Timor-Leste made an unwise decision when it chose Portuguese as its official language. This decision cut Timor-Leste off from its immediate hinterland and handicapped it economically.

Decisions about language are however not purely economic decisions. They are also decisions about our heart and soul. Mr Lee was clear about this from the very beginning. Hence in 1966, barely one year after Singapore's independence, he said categorically that "there is the necessity for preserving for each child that cultural ballast and appreciation of his origin and his background in order to give him that confidence to face the problems of his society". This commitment to "mother tongue" education is brought out well in the essay by Seng Han Thong. What is truly striking, as Seng points out, is that this commitment to support all the four languages of the Singapore community – English, Malay, Chinese and Tamil – was made way back in 1954, long before the PAP assumed office (in 1959).

It may seem simple and commonsensical to allow each minority group to speak and write its own language. Yet it is striking how many countries in the world have not allowed their minorities to use their languages. Turkey did not allow its Kurds to use their language until 2002. Indonesia did not allow its Chinese community to display Chinese characters publicly until 2000. Sri Lanka developed internal strife with its fatal decision to use only one language, Sinhalese, in 1956, instead of allowing its Tamil minority the simple right to use its own language. Imagine the amount of internal strife that could have been avoided if other countries had emulated Singapore's policy of allowing each minority to speak its own mother tongue.

The point is worth explaining as many Singaporeans, especially young Singaporeans, are not aware that Singapore could have gone down several different paths of history if some key decisions were not made as far back as the 1950s. There is one simple fact that every Singaporean should be made aware of. The British left behind many multiracial colonies in all corners of the earth. The list includes Fiji, Singapore, Sri Lanka, Cyprus and Guyana. Singapore is the only multiracial ex-British colony to avoid major internal strife. Hence, the relative political calm and multiracial harmony that Singapore has enjoyed is not a natural phenomenon.

The essay by Janadas Devan is thus an especially important contribution to this volume. Devan vigorously challenges the notion that Singapore's success could be attributed to a mechanical focus on getting the different parts of government right. He quotes from Dr Henri Ghesquiere's well-known work, *Singapore's Success*, where he says: "The political elite's passionate pursuit of shared prosperity required assembling together many diverse components ... to create an intricate and highly effective mechanism."[1]

Instead of taking a mechanical approach, the Singapore leaders took a moral approach. After quoting Dr Goh Keng Swee's famous pithy statement, "You do good, you will be rewarded. You do wrong, you will be punished," Devan goes on to argue:

> I'm convinced this simple moral regime explains the choices Mr Lee and his colleagues made in Singapore's formative years. They made the right choices because they, and the people they led, were animated by a set of values that made possible correct political, economic and social choices. Leadership – for there was nothing automatic about translating inherited values into viable state institutions – consisted of insisting on the primacy of those values and refusing to compromise on them.
>
> You do good – don't accept bribes, don't run up huge fiscal debts, don't take the easy way out – you will be rewarded. You do wrong – compromise on meritocracy, give way to atavistic impulses, promise people freebies – you will be punished.

Equally importantly, Devan's essay goes on to point out that Singapore came close to not emerging as a nation. Today, it is inconceivable to most Singaporeans that Singapore could not have existed as an independent nation state. Yet the inconceivable was a perfectly conceivable event. Indeed, a few fateful decisions in Kuala Lumpur could have delivered a very different

17

history for Singapore. Any young Singaporean who wants to understand what that alternative history might have been for Singapore need visit only one state: Penang. It may be run by an opposition party but its destiny will be determined in Kuala Lumpur. The independence of Singapore is as much a result of luck as it is of skill, indeed extraordinary geopolitical skill.

If an average Singaporean is asked today what he or she sees as the biggest challenges facing Singapore in the next 50 years, the reply will include a long list of items. Few will mention however that one of the biggest challenges that Singapore will face is how it can preserve the extraordinary amount of geopolitical space it has accumulated when the extraordinary geopolitical skills of its founding fathers are replaced by the excellent geopolitical skills of succeeding leaders. Having good geopolitical skills is an asset but since the challenges facing Singapore are extraordinary, the big question is whether excellent geopolitical skills will be enough.

The essays of Prof Chan Heng Chee and Bilahari Kausikan are important contributions that go some way toward addressing this point. Mr Lee's geopolitical skills have been carefully studied and analysed by many foreign scholars, including most recently by Graham Allison and Robert Blackwill, as well as by Tom Plate. However, no Singaporean who has worked closely with Mr Lee has tried to distil his views on geopolitics from a Singaporean's perspective. The Singaporean perspective is important because Mr Lee was remarkably focused on defending Singapore's interests even as he spoke and commented on major geopolitical trends. The best metaphor I can find to describe Mr Lee's skills in the geopolitical arena is to compare him to a surfer. He was aware that new waves of history were constantly arriving in Southeast Asia. He studied each wave carefully and when he was finally ready, he would surf it and use it to enhance Singapore's interests.

As American scholars dominate the discourse on international relations, the extraordinary relationship Mr Lee forged with key American leaders has been well documented. Prof Chan's essay provides new insights. It contains a revealing remark made by Michael Green, a National Security Council Senior Director of Asian Affairs in the George W Bush administration and one of the noted Asia analysts in Washington. Green "once described Singapore's role as a pilot for the US guiding the superpower or supertanker into the harbour. Singapore would tell the US 'come in, come in' or at times 'go back, go back,' because the US may be overstepping."

Prof Chan also documents the various ups and downs in the US-Singapore relationship. When Singapore decided to cane Michael Fay, the Clinton administration put Singapore into a form of cold storage. Amazingly, despite this painful episode, Bill Clinton later became a great fan of Lee Kuan Yew. Upon meeting Mr Lee for the first time in 2000, he said to his officials, "Why have I not met this man before?" Despite these ups and downs, Mr Lee never ceased to speak about the inherent strength of the United States. As Prof Chan says:

> When the US economy began its descent into spiralling deficits and debt, and the collapse of the financial institutions in 2008/2009, Mr Lee felt compelled to speak out against the declinist school, those predicting the decline of the US, because he did not subscribe to it. He remains convinced the US economy is resilient, has a wealth of creative talent and will continue to do well because it is open to receive the world's talents.

While a lot has been written about Mr Lee's views on the United States, less is known about how Mr Lee carefully anticipated the rise of China. In the mid-1990s, barely six years after Tiananmen, China was still trying to find its footing globally after having gone through a difficult period. Mr Lee understood early that countries that stood with China through those times would be remembered as good friends. Hence, a visionary proposal that he advanced in the mid-1990s was the Suzhou Industrial Park. In this project, Mr Lee offered to transfer some of Singapore's hard-earned "software" on urban management to a city in China. He was also a constant visitor to China in those years and probably had more frank conversations with senior Chinese leaders than any other leader. Given the inauspicious start with China after he rejected the gift from Premier Hua Guofeng in 1976, it is remarkable how much the Chinese leaders came to admire and respect Mr Lee. One of the most critical roles Mr Lee played at that time was to help the United States and China understand each other better.

One key point that Mr Lee would emphasise to American leaders was that China's rise was unstoppable. Hence it was in America's interest to develop a constructive long-term policy of engaging with China. However, Mr Lee had earlier counselled Washington not to appease China. The essay by Kausikan recounts a remarkable episode in US-China relations. As Kausikan says:

> In 1981, at the International Conference on Kampuchea held at the UN, the US was poised to sell out Singapore and ASEAN's interests in favour of China's interest to see a return of the Khmer Rouge regime. The then assistant secretary of state in charge of China policy attempted to bully and browbeat our foreign minister, saying that there would be "blood on the floor" if we did not relent.

I was personally present when the US delegation tried to browbeat our then foreign minister, S Dhanabalan, into backing down from our opposition to China's position. It was clear to me from that meeting that the American delegation was not used to having small states defy their will. Even though the Americans threatened to call Mr Lee, they never did. And they probably did not do so because they may have anticipated Mr Lee's tough response. As Kausikan recounts in his essay, Mr Lee made his views clear when he visited Washington a year later and told the Senate Foreign Relations Committee that America's China policy then was "amateurish". Few leaders of small states have had the gumption to criticise the United States so openly.

While Mr Lee's contributions in the geopolitical arena are well known, his contributions to the development of strong institutions of good governance are less known. It is good that Prof Jayakumar squarely addressed the myth that Mr Lee was a dictator. Dictators act in an arbitrary and capricious manner. The American writers who have compared Singapore to North Korea have got it all wrong. So did the late eminent American scholar Samuel Huntington, who predicted that all that Mr Lee had achieved in his lifetime would be buried in the grave with him. Instead, Mr Lee was a great believer in institution building, especially when it came to the civil service.

Both Peter Ho and Yong Ying-I know this well as they have directly participated in the processes of institution building. Ho's essay has some valuable quotations from Mr Lee's views on public management. For example, Mr Lee's high expectations are well captured in this brief remark: "The moment key leaders are less than incorruptible, less than stern in demanding high standards, from that moment the structure of administrative integrity will weaken, and eventually crumble. Singapore can survive only if ministers and senior officers are incorruptible and efficient." Yong's essay builds on Ho's essay by describing how various institutions were built with specific goals in mind. In the labour relations area, for example, his goal was to overcome the adversarial culture that Singapore had inherited from British rule. Hence, Mr Lee encouraged the creation of Labour Courts. When the Ministry of Manpower wanted to introduce escalating court charges, Mr Lee reminded the Ministry that the purpose of the court was to encourage dispute settlement, not discourage it. This is why Yong pithily observes: "My personal learning point from that was that institutionalisation of systems and processes requires subsequent generations of civil servants to understand the roots of our approaches, and what has made us successful so that we don't inadvertently dismantle them." Yong also describes well the key principles Mr Lee followed in his public policies: "Mr Lee believes in 'getting the economics right'. This included living within one's means; getting value for money from our purchases; keeping subsidies limited; not protecting weak performers; frowning on cross-subsidies which fudge true costs."

Yong also includes some personal insights about Mr Lee in her essay. So too does Minister Heng Swee Keat's essay. One memorable insight provided by Heng relates to the "so question". As he notes, Mr Lee's favourite question was "So?" This is perhaps the defining characteristic of Mr Lee's thought: throughout his political career – and as I learnt from my personal experience of dealing with him – he never ceased to question and challenge all the observations made to him.

There is also no doubt that many Singaporeans, including senior Singaporeans, felt intimidated in dealing with Mr Lee. This is why it may be best to conclude this essay with a mention of the role of Kwa Geok Choo, Mr Lee's wife. When she sensed Heng's nervousness when he was serving as PPS to Mr Lee, she said to him: "My husband has strong views but don't let that intimidate you." When I travelled several times with Mr and Mrs Lee on overseas trips, I also saw firsthand how she would gently moderate him when he expressed himself very strongly. This is why, when the final assessment of Mr Lee is done in Singapore, an equal amount of attention should be paid to the contributions of Mrs Lee. There is no doubt that Mr Lee is a great man. There is also no doubt that Mrs Lee played a critical role in making him a great man.

*Kishore Mahbubani*

23

## Endnotes

1 Henri Ghesquiere, *Singapore's Success: Engineering Economic Growth* (Singapore: Thomson Learning, 2007), p. 7.

PART
1

# PERSONAL REMINISCENCES

# Unique Experiences

*SR Nathan*

# The "So" Question

*Heng Swee Keat*

# UNIQUE EXPERIENCES

———

*SR Nathan*

MY EARLIEST MEMORY of Lee Kuan Yew dates back to the early 1950s, when I was a student. He was sitting in the audience at a public debate in Singapore organised by the University of Malaya. He had recently returned from his studies in London. His charisma was evident even at that early age. He struck me as being extraordinarily alert, a force to be reckoned with. My reflections and impressions of the man, what he has done and how he has done what he wanted, remain etched in my mind, have stayed with me since my NTUC days in the 1960s. He gave me, a junior civil servant, many assignments beyond my status.

## A FEARLESS ADVOCATE

He came onto our scene with the reputation he had made in the "Malayan Forum" in London. Later, while handling the postal workers strike in Singapore, he came to prominence locally. In the 50 years I have worked with him, what do I make of the man? Overall – his obsession was always with Singapore and his deep anxiety about our future. But there was always his confidence that, if we worked together, we would overcome whatever dangers threatened us. Perhaps this explains why he has always been fearless in advocating our cause and fighting against the odds, be this communist intimidation or chauvinism. He gave us the courage, as a people, to stand up and have the strength to fight at a time when most of us were cowed by such threats and intimidation. Back then we faced a bleak future. When independence came, we were in a region where nationalistic neighbours were determined to cut Singapore off from the middleman role that we had traditionally performed. To survive, he exhorted us to create a Singapore different from our neighbours. Singapore is now a brand name, sought after by others. We are viewed as a capable people, honest in our dealings and hardworking. This was not the case when self-government came to us in 1959 and independence in 1965. This is what he wanted us to be.

It was around the mid-1950s that he became active in our local political scene, beginning with his election to the Legislative Assembly. This was also when he began to foray overseas, taking part in political events and gatherings abroad. With such active participation abroad he started bringing Singapore to the attention of peoples and leaders, way beyond our shores, particularly among important political circles elsewhere. We were then a colony, yet he made us look like a country at such gatherings. Later in the 1960s, travelling in Africa and to New Delhi and Rangoon, he conveyed a sense of Singapore and its aspirations. Singapore thus got itself catapulted into people's consciousness, particularly among leaders in Africa and the important political centres of Asia. During those times, he even brought prominent Afro-Asian personalities to visit Singapore and speak at public forums – for instance, Ferhat Abbas, the Algerian leader, who spoke from the steps of City Hall. From my own experience attending the Afro-Asian People's Solidarity Organisation's (AAPSO) Convention, I found the foundation he had built most helpful. And all this was well before we became part of Malaysia and later independent, in 1965.

*SR Nathan*

27

The African leaders I met at the AAPSO Convention were all conscious of Singapore and Mr Lee's name was what they all linked to Singapore. Their response was immediate. I met Ben Bella of Algeria, Ahmed Sékou Touré of Guinea, Julius Nyerere of Tanzania, and they all seemed to have a special place for him. Their exclamation at the mention of "Singapore" and their responses helped open many doors for me at the conference. Mr Lee's name and reputation also had an effect on a wider stage. For example, when the Commonwealth met in Singapore in 1971, there was the danger of the conference breaking up over arms sales to South Africa. It was his standing in the eyes of African leaders that helped the conference avert a collapse.

## A LIFELONG COMMITMENT TO MULTIRACIALISM

His other cardinal contribution to us is none other than his resolve and
28  commitment to multiracialism as the principle on which our nation stands. It was not something he adopted out of political expediency. A strong commitment to multiracialism has been his creed since his student days in London. Way back in 1950, speaking to the Malayan Forum in London while still a student, he had this message for Malayan and Singaporean students:

> The prerequisite of Malayan independence is the existence of a Malayan society, not Malay, not Malayan Chinese, not Malayan Indian, not Malayan Eurasian, but Malayan, one that embraces the various races already in the country.[1]

Later, at independence, he said almost the same thing, speaking of the Singapore he wanted to see:

We are going to have a multiracial nation in Singapore. We will set the example. This is not a Malay nation, this is not a Chinese nation, this is not an Indian nation. Everybody will have his place equal: language, culture, religion. One thing we should not do is to try and stifle the other man's culture, his language, his religion, because that is the surest way to bring him to abandon reason and rationality and stand by his heritage.[2]

He has preached multiracialism ever since and put it into practice. During Singapore's days as part of Malaysia he tried to convince all Malaysians of the value of that philosophy. Unfortunately, that message was misunderstood and led to Singapore's expulsion. Since independence, multiracialism has been our creed. At independence he did not succumb to the temptation of adhering to those who advocated catering to the wishes of the majority in terms of language and race. He stood determined to uphold his belief in multiracialism in language, religion and politics. Thus, nearly 50 years later, he continues to be steadfast in practising what he had earlier preached – multiracial Singapore. From his earliest days in politics he realised that Singaporean politics must transcend racial lines and a small country like ours could not be divided against itself. He remained committed to the practice of multiracialism and we are the beneficiaries of his decision.

Some of the other essays in this volume will address the issue of Mr Lee's role in Singapore's diplomacy, and how he enlarged Singapore's international space. Therefore I will not cover this ground. But I want to make an observation relating to it. When Mr Lee created this space for Singapore, he was very clear in pointing out to the big powers that Singapore was different from them and others. We had our own system – we would be no one's lackey and we had to be accepted on these terms. Let me recount for you an incident from an earlier era, which reinforced this conviction and left a deep impression on me. It occurred in 1976 during Mr Lee's first official visit to China. During a meeting with the Chinese Premier, Hua Guofeng, Mr Lee was given a copy of a book by an Australian academic, Neville Maxwell, on the Sino-Indian War of 1962. Hua Guofeng presented the book, telling Mr Lee that "this is the correct version of the India-China war". I was sitting quite close to Prime Minister Lee and Foreign Minister Rajaratnam – perhaps in the row behind. When the PM took the book, he looked at the front and back cover and then handed it back to Premier Hua, saying: "Mr Prime Minister, this is your version of the war. There is another version, the Indian version. And in any case I am from Southeast Asia – it's nothing to do with us." Hua showed no reaction but a silence fell in the room. Madam Zhang Hanzhi, an important functionary on the Chinese side, got up and walked away. Her husband, Chao Kuan Hua, the Chinese foreign minister who was some seats away in the same row, was seen abruptly putting away the paper he was holding. I may be exaggerating, but it seemed he showed a sign of displeasure. There was silence for a while and then the conversation resumed.

That response by the PM touched me immensely. Before the meeting, for two or three days we had been shown the sights of Beijing to impress upon us the greatness of China. To do such a thing at that first official meeting with another of Chinese origin was something no one could have expected. I was moved by the way Mr Lee handed back the book, and what he said. This confirmed to me that Mr Lee might be ethnically Chinese but was not subordinate to China. Even to this day I sometimes get asked about this incident by people who cannot bring themselves to believe that the prime minister of a small country like Singapore would have dared to incur Chinese displeasure with such a response.

## GOVERNANCE WITHOUT HANDS-ON EXPERIENCE

Another area where his contributions have received worldwide acclaim has been his ability to govern our small "red dot" and transform it. He has made Singapore what it is in the eyes of today's world. In my earlier career, and later as president, I have frequently been asked how he did it. Frankly, it is not easy for any of us to explain. Short of hearing from him, none of us will be able to hazard a guess. All I can say is that he learnt on the job as things progressed.

He was a budding lawyer, successful in his profession, when he entered politics. He entered government with no experience of either government or corporate life. He had never worked in the government, or been part of a statutory board, bank or corporate leadership, so where did he learn to govern? That question is hard to answer. But, as he entered politics, right from the outset it was evident to people like me that he and his colleagues – pioneers such as Dr Goh Keng Swee, Toh Chin Chye, Yong Nyuk Lin, Lim Kim San and Ong Pang Boon – were learning on the job, and were going to transform the machinery of government.

He was always determined to intervene in administration and change not only policies, but also the way they were implemented, how they impacted our people and how they might serve them better. From the day he took office, he seemed to know how to lead us as a people and bring about change. In doing so, he brought to bear the qualities of his personal character, making observers feel he was born to lead.

*SR Nathan*

31

From the time he came into our lives, he engaged our dreams, mobilised our energies and led us towards the "promised land" that he believed was within our reach. He had the will to move us, believing he could rouse the people to take up the challenge. He seemed so sure he knew how to do it.

When he took office he quickly understood the realities of the situation confronting Singapore. Inheriting a collapsing economy, he worked closely with Dr Goh and grew our economy into the dynamic one we have today – not always with a light hand. With each year of experience he made difficult decisions, moving us away from our entrepôt dependency, applying the values of science and technology to upgrade our economy, making it what it is today. He did all this by studying the experience of others and drawing lessons from their successes and failures.

Since independence in 1965, everything he did or said was subordinated to one thing – the survival of Singapore and its people. He has always urged us to prepare ourselves to confront the dangers ahead in an ever changing, often turbulent world.

When we gained independence, Singapore was not fully formed as a country or a nation. We entered the international area to take our place among established nations. Many sceptics doubted we would survive. It was his reassuring words and constant exhortations, together with the tireless work of our first foreign minister, S Rajaratnam, that gave us the strength to face the imponderable future. He navigated us through troubled waters with such skill that by the 1970s, the picture around us and within had changed dramatically.

During the rough and tumble of our early days there were shrinking alliances – some deserted us in the expectation we would fail; others stood by us and took a stand against the odds. What I will always remember is how

32

Mr Lee consistently pursued our interests, with passion and without loss of enthusiasm, no matter whether the dangers heightened or receded. He was always conscious and up to date with the political, economic and social issues facing us as a country. In a crisis, he could be impatient, wanting a quick solution. But one still left such meetings persuaded by the compelling purpose of what he was trying to achieve – be it in politics or economics. Whatever he heard he absorbed and processed in his mind with amazing speed. Whenever he wanted his interlocutors to hear something, he engaged them in such a way that their entire attention was on what he had to say. In these exchanges, he was supremely confident about what he wanted to achieve.

## PERSONAL QUALITIES

When talking about him, one has to reckon with his intelligence and remarkable grasp of things. He grasped the nature of the world Singapore found itself in and the way things were moving – for or against Singapore's interest. For this he did not depend on what we officials purveyed to him. He read widely. He was never satisfied until he understood for himself the accuracy of facts presented to him. What he did not grasp he kept probing. In this way, he absorbed information on economic and political developments, sorted them out in his mind and made sense of them before he responded.

His analytical power of addressing developing situations was spot on. He was able to get to the nub of the issue and point out to us what was vital. He also had a great ability to communicate his ideas to small and large groups. Depending on the situation, his audience might be made up of many who may not be well-versed in English. On such occasions, he would comment or criticise using a Malay or Chinese (dialect) expression that resonated with

*SR Nathan*

33

the average man and even entertained the audience.

I want to end with one observation that may surprise some of you. It is about his caring nature and my single most moving experience of it, among many others.

In 1967, I was sent as a junior officer to take notes of his meeting with the Thai foreign minister. I hurriedly put on a tie and jacket and rushed to the assignment. On my arrival at the door, the prime minister came close to me, adjusted my necktie and said, with an almost paternal touch, these words: "Nathan – you must remember you are no longer in the labour movement." I was moved beyond words.

I had grown up without a father or an elder brother. Here was the prime minister himself coming down to my level to do what they would have done for me. That instance of his caring nature, I experienced many times later in life. It is something most people do not attribute to him.

## Endnotes

1 "The Returned Student", talk by Mr Lee to the Malayan Forum at Malaya Hall, 28 January 1950. *The Papers of Lee Kuan Yew: Speeches, Interviews and Dialogues, vol. 1: 1950–1962* (Singapore: Gale Asia, 2012), p. 8.

2 Lee Kuan Yew, press conference announcing Singapore's separation from Malaysia, 9 August 1965. *The Papers of Lee Kuan Yew: Speeches, Interviews and Dialogues, vol. 3: 1965–1966* (Singapore: Gale Asia, 2012), p. 14.

# THE "SO" QUESTION

_Heng Swee Keat_

THE FIRST TIME I met Lee Kuan Yew was in March 1997 when he interviewed me for the job of principal private secretary or PPS. His questions were fast and sharp. Every reply drew even more probing questions. At the end of it, he said: "Brush up your Mandarin and report in three months. We have an important project with China."

I realised later that it was perhaps when I replied "I don't know" to one or two questions that I made an impression. With Mr Lee, it is all right if you do not know something. But do not pretend and lie if you do not know. Integrity is everything.

I had the privilege of working as Mr Lee's PPS from mid-1997 to early 2000. This was the period of the Asian financial crisis, and Mr Lee was writing his memoirs. I benefited much from interacting with him and attending his meetings with many prominent leaders. I learnt much about his worldview, about how he translates ideas into results and what he is like as a person.

## HIS WORLDVIEW

Mr Lee's worldview is comprehensive and consistent. Three strands stand out for me.

The first is about Singapore's place in the world. He has experienced wars and foreign domination, sung four different national anthems in his lifetime and fought for Singapore's independence. Naturally, Mr Lee's lifelong preoccupation is how Singapore, a resource-poor city-state, can survive in a world where powers big and small compete for supremacy.

His view is that a small city-state can best survive in a benign world environment, where there is a balance of powers, where no single state dominates and where the rule of law prevails in international affairs. A small city-state has to stay open and connect with all nations and economic powerhouses. To prosper, Singapore has to be relevant to the world. We must be exceptional.

Second, his views about human nature, culture and society. Some societies are more successful than others because of the way they are organised, and the values and cultures that underpin them. As human beings we have two sides to our nature – one that is selfish, that seeks to compete and to maximise benefits for ourselves, our families, our clans; the other that is altruistic, that seeks to cooperate, to help others and to contribute to the common good. A society loses its vigour if it eschews excellence and competition; equally, a society loses its cohesion if it fails to take care of those who are left behind or disadvantaged. Mr Lee believes that this tension between competition and cooperation, between *yin* and *yang*, is one that has to be constantly recalibrated. Within a society, those who are successful must contribute back to society and help others find success. We must share the fruits of our collective efforts.

Third, his views about governance and leadership. Societies are subject to complex forces, and do not become successful automatically. As a lawyer, Mr Lee believes deeply in the rule of law and the importance of institutions in creating a good society. But institutions are only as good as the people who run them. Good governance needs leaders with the right values, a sense of service and ability. It is important to have leaders who can forge with the people the vision for the future and the way forward. Above all, leaders are stewards. They should develop future leaders and when the time comes, they should relinquish their positions so that the next generation of leaders can take us to greater heights.

## A MENTAL MAP FOCUSED ON SINGAPORE

While Mr Lee's worldview is wide-ranging and widely sought, when I worked with him, I had the privilege of learning how his views are so coherent, rigorous and fresh, and how he put his agile mind to the service of the Singapore cause. A few incidents show this clearly.

38 First, Mr Lee has a favourite question: "So?" If you update him on something, he will invariably reply with "So?" You reply and think you have answered him, but again he asks, "So?" This "So?" forces you to get to the core of the issue and draw out the implications of each fact. His instinct is to cut through the clutter, drill to the core of the issue and identify the vital points. And he does this with an economy of effort.

I learnt this the hard way. Once, in response to a question, I wrote him three paragraphs. I thought I was comprehensive. Instead, he said, "I only need a one-sentence answer, why did you give me three paragraphs?" I reflected on this, and realised that that was how he cut through clutter. When he was prime minister, it was critical to distinguish between strategic and peripheral issues.

Second, Mr Lee is intellectually open. On my first overseas trip with Mr Lee, Mrs Lee, ever so kind, must have sensed my nervousness. She said to me: "My husband has strong views, but don't let that intimidate you!" Indeed, Mr Lee has strong views because these are rigorously derived, but he is also very open to robust exchange. He makes it a point to hear from those with expertise and experience. He is persuasive, but he can be persuaded. A few months into my job, Mr Lee decided on a particular course of action on the Suzhou Industrial Park after deep discussion with our senior officials. That evening, I realised that amid the flurry of information, we had not discussed a point that was relevant to our approach. Gingerly, I wrote him a note, proposing some changes. To my surprise, he agreed.

Third, Mr Lee's rich insights on issues come from a capacious and disciplined mind. He listens and reads widely, but he does so like a detective, looking for and linking vital clues while discarding the irrelevant. Once, he asked if I recalled an old newspaper article on US-China relations. I could not – this was several months back and I had put it out of my mind – but a fresh news article had triggered him to link the two developments. I realised that he has a mental map of the world whose contours he knows well. Like a radar, he is constantly scanning for changes and matching these against the map. What might appear as random and disparate facts to many of us are placed within this map, and hence his mental map is constantly being refreshed. A senior US leader described this well: Mr Lee is like a one-man intelligence agency.

The most remarkable feature of the map in Mr Lee's head is the fact that the focal point is always Singapore. Invariably, the "So?" question ends with, "So, what does this mean for Singapore?" What are the implications? What should we be doing differently? Nothing is too big or too small. I accompanied Mr Lee on many overseas trips. The 1998 trip to the United States was particularly memorable. Each day brought new ideas, and throughout the trip I sent back many of his observations for our departments to study. It might be the type of industry that we might develop or the type of trees that might add colour to our garden city. This remains his style today.

His every waking moment is devoted to Singapore, and Mr Lee wanted Singapore to be successful beyond his term as prime minister. From the early '60s, he already spoke about finding his successor. During my term with him, when he was senior minister, he devoted much of his effort to helping then Prime Minister Goh Chok Tong succeed. He refrained from visiting Indonesia and Malaysia as he wanted PM Goh to establish himself as our leader. Instead, he fanned out to China, the United States and Europe to convince leaders and investors that PM Goh's leadership would take Singapore to new levels of success.

As senior minister, he worked out with PM Goh the areas in which he could contribute. I will share three key projects that illustrate his contribution, but more importantly, how he develops insights and achieves results.

## TURNING INSIGHTS INTO RESULTS

Insights are valuable, but how does Mr Lee turn insights into results? I believe it is through a single-minded focus on achieving whatever he sets out to do.

The Suzhou Industrial Park project was one of the areas in which PM Goh asked Mr Lee to stay actively involved. Two years into the project, we ran into teething problems. Local Chinese officials promoted their own rival park. Some felt that such start-up problems and cultural differences were to be expected and would be resolved over time. But Mr Lee drilled deep into the issues and held many meetings with our officials. He worked with an intensity that I had not expected of someone who was then 75 years old.

He concluded that the problem was much more fundamental. China had (and still has) a very complex system of government with many layers and many interest groups – some visible, some invisible. The interests of the various groups at the local levels were not aligned with the objectives that the central government in Beijing and Singapore had agreed upon. Unless this was put right, the project would not go far.

Instead of hoping that time would resolve this, Mr Lee raised issues at the highest levels, and made the disagreements public. He was unfazed that going public could diminish his personal standing. Among Mr Lee's proposals to the Chinese were two radical changes: to swap the shareholding structure so that the Chinese had majority control, and to appoint the CEO of the rival park to head the Suzhou Industrial Park. It was not a given that these changes would work. But Mr Lee was proven right – the changes created the necessary realignment and put the project back on track.

This year we will witness the 20th anniversary of Suzhou Industrial Park. From all accounts, it has been a success story, not just in its development, but also in how it has enabled a new generation of leaders from both sides to develop a deeper understanding of each other, paving the way for further collaboration.

I learnt a valuable lesson from this experience. If things go wrong, do not sweep them aside. Confront the problems, get to the root of the difficulties and wrestle with these resolutely. Go for long-term success, and do not be deterred by criticisms.

My second example, on the revamping of the financial sector, shows how Mr Lee is constantly looking out for how Singapore should change, and how he turns adversity into opportunity. The 1997/8 Asian financial crisis hit the region hard. Many analysts attributed it to cronyism, corruption and nepotism. Mr Lee read up on all the technical analyses and met with our economists. I was amazed, at the age of 75, how deeply he delved into the issues. He concluded that the reason was more basic – investors' euphoria and the weak banking and regulatory systems in the affected countries had allowed a huge influx of short-term capital. These weaknesses had their origins in the political system. Cronyism exacerbated the problems, but was not the cause. Years later, many bankers have told me that Mr Lee's analysis was the best they had heard.

Mr Lee was convinced that though Asia's economic growth had been set back temporarily, dynamism would return. In the short term, we had to navigate the crisis carefully, but for the longer term we should turn this adversity into opportunities. While investors fled, we should use the crisis to lay the foundation for a stronger Singapore in a rising Asia.

He took the opportunity to review the long-term positioning of Singapore's financial sector. With the permission of then PM Goh, he met with experts from different backgrounds as well as the chairmen of local banks. For years, Mr Lee had believed in strict regulation and in protecting our local banks. While this approach protected our banks from the crisis, it had its costs. Our stringent rules, while appropriate in the past, were now stifling growth and our banks were falling behind. He was persuaded that our regulatory stance had to change.

I was struck by Mr Lee's systematic and calibrated approach to changing a complex financial system. He has a reputation for being impatient for results and for driving a fast pace. This is true, but he is also wise in distinguishing between things that change only slowly, and things that ought to change swiftly. Instead of one big bang, he was in favour of a series of steps which added up to a significant shift of direction.

Mr Lee discussed with and sought PM Goh's approval on the broad plan to revamp the financial sector. PM Goh agreed with the plan, and later appointed then Deputy Prime Minister Lee Hsien Loong as the chairman of the Monetary Authority of Singapore (MAS) in January 1998. DPM Lee, who has a very strategic grasp of issues and pays meticulous attention to details, reviewed major policies and re-orientated MAS' organisational culture.

Remarkably, within a few years, MAS was transformed. By 2006, when I became the managing director of MAS, I inherited an organisation with a new set of regulatory doctrines and a deeper pool of talent. The global financial crisis of 2007/8 tested our system severely. We not only withstood the shock, we emerged stronger after the crisis. Singaporeans' savings were well protected and businesses recovered rapidly.

If Mr Lee had not initiated the changes in the late 1990s, and sought to turn adversity into opportunity, we would not have become a stronger financial centre today. To prepare ourselves to open up our financial system in the midst of one of the worst financial crises is to me an act of great foresight and boldness. It has the stamp of Mr Lee.

My third example relates to how Mr Lee expanded our external space, by being a principled advocate of collaboration based on long-term interests.

Today, we are remarkably well connected but this did not come about by accident. Over the years, Mr Lee has worked hard at this. His strategic worldview has projected Singapore onto the global stage and created opportunities for Singaporeans. In all his years as the face of Singapore, Mr Lee has also made fast friendships with senior world leaders who appreciate his view of things and respect Singapore's principled stance on

*Heng Swee Keat*

43

international issues. In PM Goh's time and today, Mr Lee remains a steady, respected voice in the international arena. This was driven home to me at two meetings.

In 1999, relations between the US and China were very tense. China's negotiations with the US on the former's entry to the WTO had failed, there were tensions between the US and China over US bombs that had hit the Chinese embassy in Belgrade, and President Lee Teng-hui in Taiwan had pronounced his "two states" concept. In July 1999, US Secretary of State Madeleine Albright and Chinese Foreign Minister Tang Jiaxuan were in Singapore for the ASEAN Regional Forum. The atmosphere was quite uneasy, and many of our officials believed that there could be a flare-up at the ARF. Both leaders met Mr Lee separately. He gave each side his reading of their long-term strategic interests. His advice to the US was that it was not in their interest to be adversarial towards China or regard it as a potential enemy. To China, he suggested that they should tap into the market, technology and capital of the US to develop their economy. They should look forward and search for areas of cooperation, such as China's entry into the WTO.

Sitting in these meetings, I was struck by how Mr Lee approached this delicate situation. He did not say one thing to one and sing a different tune to another. If they had compared notes later, they would have found his underlying position consistent. What made him persuasive was how he addressed the concerns and interests of each side. I could see from the way both reacted that his arguments struck a chord, and one of the guests asked a note taker to write the notes verbatim for deeper study later on. In 2000, a few months after this meeting, I was very pleased to witness China's entry into the WTO at the Doha meeting.

## MR LEE IN PERSON

What is Mr Lee like as a person? His public persona is of a stern, strict, no-nonsense leader. But deep down, he is energised by an abiding sense of care for Singaporeans, especially for the disadvantaged. He does not express this in soft, sentimental terms – his policies speak louder and he is content to let them speak for themselves. He distributed the fruits of Singapore's progress in a very significant way by enabling Singaporeans to own their flats. Apart from the investment in education, he donated generously to the Education Fund, which provides awards, especially to outstanding students from poor families. He is a firm advocate for a fair and just society. But he demands that everyone, including those who are helped, put in their fair share of effort.

Many regard Mr Lee as a pragmatist who does not hesitate to speak hard truths. Actually, I think he is also an idealist with a deep sense of purpose. He believes one has to see the world as it is, not as one wishes it to be. Fate deals us a certain hand, but it is up to us to make a winning hand out of it. Through sheer will, conviction and imagination, there is always hope of progress. Man is not perfect, but we can be better. Mr Lee embraces Confucianism because of its belief in the perfectibility of man. No society is perfect either, but a society with a sense of togetherness can draw out the best of our human spirit and create a better future for our people. He is to me a pragmatic idealist.

During my term as PPS, the prime minister of a Pacific Island nation asked to call on Mr Lee. Given Mr Lee's very tight schedule, I thought he would not be able to meet him. To my surprise, Mr Lee said he would make the time. He explained that this young prime minister's father had been a comrade in arms, fighting the British for independence, and he owed it to his father (who had passed on) to offer whatever advice might be useful.

Mr Lee and his family are closely knit, and he was particularly close to Mrs Lee. On overseas trips, I had the opportunity to have many private meals with them. It was heartwarming to see their bantering. Mr Lee has a sweet tooth and Mrs Lee would with good humour keep score of the week's "ration". But when it came to official work, they drew very clear lines. Mrs Lee stayed close by Mr Lee's side and travelled with him whenever she could.

Once, in Davos, Mrs Lee came into the tiny room where Mr Lee was giving a media interview. She found a stool at the corner and sat there, listening unobtrusively. Twice, I offered her my more comfortable seat near Mr Lee. She said to me: "You have work to do. I am just a busybody – don't let me disturb you!" Mrs Lee was supportive, without intruding – she was certainly not "just a busybody", and anyone who had the chance to observe them together would know just how close a couple they were, and how much strength her presence gave to her husband.

## AN UNWAVERING DEDICATION TO SINGAPORE

We live today in a different world that demands of us new ideas and approaches. But there is one quality of Lee Kuan Yew's that we can, and need to, aspire towards: his unwavering and total dedication to Singapore, to keeping Singapore successful so that Singaporeans may determine their own destiny and lead meaningful, fulfilling lives.

Singapore's survival and success are Mr Lee's life's work and his lifelong preoccupation. History gave him a most daunting challenge – building a nation out of a tiny city-state with no resources and composed of disparate migrants. He cast aside his doubts, mustered all his being and has given it his all. Mr Lee's most significant achievement is to show the way forward in building a nation. There were and still are no textbook answers for achieving this. Mr Lee and his team analysed the issues from first principles and had the courage and conviction to do what was right and what would work for Singapore. He and his team would try, adapt and experiment, to get on with the job of making Singapore a better home for all.

In the same way that he asks himself, we need to always be asking ourselves, "So?" So what does this mean for Singapore? So what should we do about it? Of the many qualities I have observed in Mr Lee, this is the one that leaves the deepest impression on me, the one that I hope we can learn.

We take inspiration from the courage and determination of Mr Lee and his colleagues. The task of creating a better life for all Singaporeans – through expanding opportunities and through building a fair and just society – never ends. Mr Lee is not just a man of ideas; he is a man of action. I hope that this volume will not only enable us to understand Lee Kuan Yew's ideas; I hope it also stirs us to action with the same unwavering dedication to Singapore and our future.

*Heng Swee Keat*

47

PART
2

# LAW AND POLITICS

## Lee Kuan Yew and The Rule of Law

*Chan Sek Keong*

## Order and Law? Lee Kuan Yew and The Rule of Law

*S Jayakumar*

# LEE KUAN YEW
# AND THE RULE OF LAW

*Chan Sek Keong*

## INTRODUCTION

SINCE 1962, MR LEE has made many speeches and given many more interviews on economic and political developments in Singapore and Asia in which he has referred to the "rule of law" more than a hundred times. No government leader in history is likely to have spoken more often on the subject of the rule of law.

How has this come about? As Mr Lee has been the moving force and chief architect of the spectacular transformation of Singapore from a Third World to a First World country, his advice on how he did it and whether other countries could use his model has been sought far and wide. His standard response has invariably been to refer to the rule of law as a contributory factor, alongside other factors such as good government and sound policies, efficient public services and low corruption.

However, Mr Lee has never on these occasions explained fully to his audience what he means by the rule of law. He took for granted that the audience understood what the term meant. He made his first public speech on the rule of law in 1962, but by then, there were already various conceptions of the rule of law in the global marketplace of ideas or ideologies.

Therefore, to appreciate fully Mr Lee's approach to the rule of law, it is necessary we also understand his conception of the rule of law. In this essay I shall endeavour to do only two things. First, I will discuss what Mr Lee's "rule of law" means. Second, I will compare its merits with those of other competing conceptions of the rule of law, to show that criticisms of Mr Lee's rule of law, mostly from foreign critics, are misguided. Let me start by giving a very short summary of the rule of law, past and present.

## THE RULE OF LAW: PAST AND PRESENT

The rule of law has always been associated with how society is or should be governed. Hence, as a principle of government, it is of ancient origin – going back more than 2,000 years to Aristotle's political philosophy that "it is more proper that the law should govern than any of its citizens".[1] The fundamental idea is that the more arbitrary power the government has, the less freedom the people have, and vice versa. The modern use of the phrase "government by laws and not by men" can be traced to this statement.[2]

The development of the modern rule of law in England was inspired by the signing of the Magna Carta in 1215 by King John.[3] The Great Charter signified "a clear rejection of unbridled and unaccountable royal powers, an assertion that even the supreme power of the state must be subject to certain overriding rules".[4] By the middle of the 19th century, the principle that executive power is subject to the law was well established in England, and consequently in Singapore too, as it was a British colony.

In 1855, AV Dicey, an Oxford law professor, published his classic *An Introduction to the Study of the Law of the Constitution*.[5] In his book, Dicey gave three meanings to "the rule of law":

(a)   the supremacy of the law over arbitrary power;

(b)   equality before the law; and

(c)   the general principles of the constitution (such as individual rights) were found in decisions of the courts based on common law.

It should be noted that Dicey's rule of law says nothing about the morality or fairness of the law. The law can be oppressive or unjust, but Dicey assumed that English law was fundamentally moral and just, the common law being based on reason and morality derived mainly from Christian principles and values.

For the next 90 years, Dicey's rule of law was the accepted and orthodox principle of government in Western democracies. However, the principle of liberty (that a person cannot be deprived of his liberty except by a court after a fair trial according to its established procedures) had to be qualified during World War II (WWII) when Britain enacted the Defence of the Realm Act (1939–1942) (popularly termed DORA) to detain persons of German origin without trial. After WWII, the Allied Powers, led by the United States, founded the United Nations in 1948 to promote international security, economic development, social progress, civil rights and liberties, political freedoms and democracy and peace in the world. The Universal Declaration of Human Rights 1948 declared that human rights should be protected by "the rule of law" so that the people would not need to resort to rebellion against tyranny and oppression. Building on this aspiration, a conference organised by the International Commission of Jurists issued the 1959 Delhi Declaration as follows:

The Rule of Law is a dynamic concept ... which should be employed not only to safeguard and advance the civil and political rights of the individual in a free society, but also to establish social, economic, educational and cultural conditions under which legitimate aspirations and dignity may be realised.[6]

This definition is so vague and all-embracing that the rule of law ceases to be a meaningful concept.

In the 1980s, the developed economies of Western democracies began the process of globalising trade and investments. American triumphalism after the collapse of the Soviet Union in the Cold War and the opening up of China's economy led the US liberal democratic establishment to revive the rule of law to support economic development in Russia, China and other developing countries, and to advance the cause of liberal democracy.[7] This is a "liberal" conception of the rule of law that incorporates the values of liberal democracy and the concept of human rights, as distinguished from the "thin" conception, of which Dicey's rule of law is an example.

The US promoted this liberal rule of law as the political ideal to which every country in the world should aspire. The World Bank spent billions of dollars in trying to develop the rule of law around the world, but with "limited success".[8]

The idea that emerging economies in Asia, the Middle East and Latin America – with their different histories, cultures and values – would adopt the liberal rule of law as their political ideal was a non-starter. The matter was not so simple. As Mr Lee put it:

The rule of law is a change in mental approach, not only of judges and lawyers but of the population and the government.[9]

This is where the rule of law stands today – contested by legal and political philosophers according to which legal theory, social philosophy or political ideology they subscribe to. However, as Mr Lee does not subscribe to any particular political philosophy other than pragmatism as a principle of government, his view of the rule of law has both elements of the "liberal" and "thin" versions. It may be said that Mr Lee's conception of the rule of law prioritises order over what he regards as excessive individual liberties and rights. His conception is calibrated to provide a fine balance between the security of the state and individual rights.

## LEE KUAN YEW'S RULE OF LAW – THE 1962 SPEECH

In 1962, when Mr Lee made his first speech on the rule of law, the Preservation of Public Security Ordinance 1955 (or "PPSO", which re-enacted substantially the 1948 Emergency Regulations) was still in force in Singapore.[10] The PPSO provided for detention without trial. This speech sets out Mr Lee's philosophy that the rule of law is more than simply the law of rules.

On 18 January 1962, Mr Lee spoke to the University of Singapore Law Society on the subject "Law and Order, Justice and Fair Play".[11] Here are the material extracts:

(1) There is a gulf between the principles of the rule of law... and its actual practice in contemporary Britain. The gulf is even wider between the principle and its practical application in the hard realities of the social and economic conditions of Malaya. ...

(2)   The rule of law talks of habeas corpus, freedom, the right of association and expression, of assembly, of peaceful demonstration... But nowhere in the world today are these rights allowed to practise without limitations, for blindly applied, these ideals can work toward the undoing of organised society. For the acid test of any legal system is not the greatness or the grandeur of its ideal concepts, but whether in fact it is able to produce order and justice in the relationships between man and man, and between man and the state.

(3)   In a settled and established society, law appears to be a precursor of order. Good laws lead to good order. But... without order, the operation of law is impossible. Order having been established and the rules having become enforceable in a settled society, only then is it possible to work out human relationships between subject and subject, and subject and the state in accordance with predetermined rules of law.

(4)   And when a state of increasing disorder and defiance of authority cannot be checked by the rules then existing, new and sometimes drastic rules have to be forged to maintain order so that the law can continue to govern human relations. The alternative is to surrender order for chaos and anarchy. So it is that we have to allow the use of extraordinary powers of detention, first in the case of political offenders under the PPSO and next in the case of secret society gangsters under the Criminal Law (Temporary Provisions) Ordinance (CLTPO).

(5)   These extraordinary powers do not measure well against the ideals of habeas corpus and the precedents of individual liberty in two

*Chan Sek Keong*

55

centuries of peaceful non-revolutionary England. But the sociological and political conditions in which we find ourselves make it vital that there should be radical departures from English patterns.

(6)   The realities of the sociological and political milieu in Malaya and of the world of 1962 are that if you allow these shibboleths of "law and order" to be uttered out of context and without regard to the actual social and political conditions we are in, you may unwittingly make these words your own undoing. For in the last analysis if the state disintegrates then the rules of all laws must vanish.

(7)   Justice and fair play according to predetermined rules of law can be achieved within our situation if there is integrity of purpose and an intelligent search for forms which will work and which will meet the needs of our society. Reality is relatively more fixed than form. So, if we allow form to become fixed because reality cannot be so easily varied, then calamity must befall us.

Mr Lee's 1962 speech was primarily a defence of the need for the PPSO. But, he also made several other important points. First, the law must serve the needs of society. If it does not, it must be adapted or changed to do so. Second, the law must reflect reality. If it does not, it must be adapted and changed to do so. Otherwise, the law, if blindly applied, could lead to "our undoing", i.e. it could undermine order and security, or lead to injustice. These principles permeated his philosophy of law and politics. "The law is a tool that can hinder or facilitate social reform" and bring about "progress and cultural change. It is not a sacrosanct set of principles, but is one of the means by which society transforms itself, defines itself and evolves."[12]

Mr Lee's rule of law, from what he has said in his speeches and interviews, consists of the following propositions:

(1)    The state may only exercise power in accordance with the law, i.e. the procedures, principles and constraints in the law.

(2)    Everyone is equal before the law, and equally subject to the law, and any citizen can find redress against any other, including the government, for any act which involves a breach of the law.

(3)    The purpose of the rule of law is to produce order and justice in the relationships between man and man, and between man and the state. Hence, the rule of law:

(a)    requires that judges be independent so that they can decide disputes impartially and without interference from any party, including, but especially, the government.

(b)    is necessary to protect the integrity and sovereignty of the state and maintain law and order so as to create an orderly and safe environment where people can live in safety, peace and harmony, and to that end,

*i*    detention-without-trial laws are justified if used for those ends;

*ii*    penalties and punishments must also be appropriate and effective to achieve those ends;

*iii*    the law must be strictly enforced;

(c)    requires the state to enact laws that *inter alia* promote

*i*    social stability and economic growth;

*Chan Sek Keong*

57

*ii*  racial and religious harmony;

*iii*  and deter all acts and activities harmful to the people
and the state, including corruption, trafficking in drugs
and in women and children, etc.

(4)  The rule of law (having these characteristics) is an economic asset
as it provides a stable and safe environment for foreign investments.

(5)  The rule of law is essential to the international order as it will
prevent aggression against small and vulnerable states and there will
be peaceful co-existence and stability in the international order.

Mr Lee has stated in an interview that he regarded the rule of law as the
most valuable legacy that the British left to Singapore. Nevertheless, he did
not consider it as sufficient for building a successful nation. In an interview
with Tom Plate, Mr Lee said:

I don't believe just having a sound constitution, the rule of law and
institutions will make Singapore continue successfully. You need good
men to run it, to improve on it, to adjust and change as the international
situation changes, and as the domestic needs become different.[13]

Mr Lee is, of course, right. Laws are made by man. We no longer believe
in divine law as a source of law. Laws are not self-executing, and legal
institutions are not self-operational. Laws have to be applied and enforced
by people. The law is a means to an end. It can serve a good end or an evil
end. A legal philosopher has used the analogy of a knife – it can be used

to carve roast or to kill people.[14] Good people make good laws and good laws will create the necessary conditions for good people to make a country successful.

## FOREIGN CRITICISMS OF MR LEE'S RULE OF LAW AND RESPONSES

In spite of Singapore's success under Mr Lee's rule of law, Singapore has been regularly criticised for having no rule of law. Here are two typical examples. In 2007 the Lawyers' Rights Watch Canada, an NGO, published a report on the rule of law in Singapore which concluded as follows:

> A number of factors amply demonstrate that Singapore is not governed by the rule of law. The factors include: a demonstrated lack of independence of lawyers to stand between the state and the citizen without fear of reprisals, inadequate statutory safeguards of the independence of the judiciary, a perception of executive influence over the judiciary in cases involving PAP interest, the stifling of public debate regarding issues of public importance through laws restricting freedom of assembly and freedom of expression to a degree incompatible with democracy, the threat of arbitrary arrest and detention through use of the ISA, and the use, by members of the executive and the PAP, of defamation to punish and incapacitate government critics and members of opposition parties.[15]

A second example is the report issued by the Human Rights Institute of the International Bar Association (IBAHRI) in July 2008, following IBA's 2007 conference in Singapore where Mr Lee delivered the opening address and explained to members of the IBA how and why the rule of law was indispensable to Singapore's success.[16] The IBAHRI report concluded:

> A strong and robust rule of law requires respect for and protection of democracy, human rights – including freedom of speech and freedom of assembly – and an independent and impartial judiciary. The IBAHRI is concerned that, despite many positive achievements, the Singapore government is currently failing to meet established international standards in these areas.[17]

To remedy this alleged failure, IBAHRI called on the Singapore government to implement its 18 recommendations which were concerned largely with freedom of expression, press freedom, defamation (civil and criminal) and internet speech.

These criticisms are directed not at Mr Lee's rule of law, but his rejection of the values of Western liberal democracy and its notion of human rights. They conflate liberal democracy and human rights with the rule of law in order to give the appearance of criticising Mr Lee's rule of law. To Mr Lee, the rule of law is not democracy, although democracy cannot exist without the rule of law.[18] To Mr Lee, the rule of law is not human rights,[19] although human rights cannot be enjoyed without the rule of law to establish and protect them. What the ideal form of democracy is for nations at certain stages of their social and economic development is a contested idea. But neither liberal democracy nor human rights is a necessary condition for economic success.

Mr Lee does not believe that Western liberal democracy is the best system of government for Singapore, given its circumstances. He has never confused the rule of law with the form of democracy and human rights promoted by Western democratic liberals. But that does not mean that he does not respect the value of democracy and *fundamental* human rights, i.e. rights that define or are inherent in a human being – to live, to think, to speak, to associate with fellow human beings, to work, to move about, to procreate and, equally important, not to be harmed by others. Many such rights are constitutional rights in Singapore. But the exercise of those rights is subject to the larger interests of the community. It is basically a question of balancing security of the state with individual liberties. The disagreement is on where the line should be drawn.

Mr Lee rejects allegations that the proper use of the Internal Security Act (ISA) is an infringement of individual right to liberty. He does not consider that detaining without trial people who are a threat to the security of Singapore or the safety of its people is a breach of the detainee's constitutional liberty. There is no human right or constitutional right to do harm to people and society. On the contrary, there is a social obligation not to do so. To Mr Lee, the responsible use of the ISA protects the state and the people from harm. Detention without trial is not contrary to his concept of the rule of law.

Singapore's situation under Mr Lee's rule of law is indeed quite ironic. Singapore has been constantly criticised for its weak or oppressive rule of law. Yet, if all the rights and privileges enjoyed by Singaporeans in terms of social welfare, and a standard of living that takes into account housing, education, health and medical care, transport, recreation, all the infrastructural needs of an advanced society – all of which are desired goals of the liberal conception of the rule of law – Singaporeans are actually better off under Mr Lee's rule of law and enjoy more societal goods or rights than people in many countries

*Chan Sek Keong*

claiming to have the ideal or liberal rule of law.

Mr Lee's conception of the rule of law is therefore seen by many as a competitor of the liberal conception of the rule of law in the global marketplace of ideas or ideologies in the area of good governance. Mr Lee's model is not without its admirers in many states. Most foreign criticisms emanate from Western liberal democracies and are usually directed not at Mr Lee's rule of law as such, but its liberal democratic deficit in individual liberties because of the Internal Security Act (ISA) and because ministers of the government exercise their civil rights to sue their political opponents for defamation. These criticisms merit some discussion.

## DETENTION WITHOUT TRIAL – THE INTERNAL SECURITY ACT

The first criticism is that detention without trial is contrary to the rule of law as the detainee has not been convicted of an offence after a trial in a court of law. Mr Lee justifies the government's resort to detention without trial to protect national security because the ordinary legal process is incapable of securing conviction of those who are the greatest threats to national security. Few people in Singapore would complain if the ISA is used, as it is being used, against jihadists, terrorists and like-minded anarchists. The problem is how to balance the needs of national security with the constitutional or civil rights of the detainee. It is interesting to note that there has been scant or no foreign criticism of the Criminal Law (Temporary Provisions) Act, which has made Singapore one of the safest countries in the world in terms of personal security. The balance can be achieved in providing administrative and judicial safeguards to ensure that the power of detention is not abused and that the detainee is not detained arbitrarily.

The crux of foreign criticisms against the ISA is that it allows for arbitrary

62

arrest and indefinite detention of the government's political opponents and critics without reasonable cause, and that the courts have no legal power to intervene. Because the ISA is an arbitrary law, it is not only a threat to individual liberties, but also to freedom of speech, and more importantly, to the normal development of the political process and the growth of democratic opposition to the government *du jour*. As a matter of law, these criticisms are not justified as the ISA does not allow or permit arbitrary arrest and detention. If opposition politicians in the past felt intimidated by the ISA, and did not speak out against the government on political issues of the day because of fear of being detained under the ISA, I would suggest that such fear was borne out of a misunderstanding of their constitutional rights and the rule of law in Singapore.

Firstly, the ISA does not sanction arbitrary detention, without reason or capriciously, at the whim of the government. The ISA requires the detainee be served the grounds of detention. The grounds have to relate to national security. Secondly, although the subjective satisfaction of the President that a detainee is a threat to national security may not be questioned by the detainee or reviewed by the court, the detainee is entitled to challenge the allegations of fact against him and disprove their truth or relevance to national security. The President has no legal power to detain a person under the ISA on his *ipse dixit* (on his say so). For instance, the President may not detain a person under the ISA on the basis that: "I believe you are a terrorist, and for that reason I am satisfied your actions are prejudicial to national security."[20] There must be words uttered or actions done by the detainee that are capable of causing such prejudice. Thirdly, the criticism that the ISA allows indefinite detention is also not correct. A person may only be detained if he is, or remains, a threat to national security. The moment the detainee ceases to be so, he has a right to be released – to secure which he can apply to the court for an order directing the government to release him immediately.

Finally, it is also not correct to allege that the court has no legal power to intervene and to set aside an unlawful detention apparently on national security grounds under the ISA. The court has a constitutional duty to determine whether the detainee has been deprived of his liberty according to law.[21] The ISA confers extensive but not unfettered powers on the executive. If the grounds of detention show or are proven to be extraneous to national security, the detention order is outside the purpose of the ISA, and therefore unlawful. The court has the power to set aside a detention order which has no factual basis as regards the grounds of detention.

In his 1962 speech, Mr Lee referred to "integrity of purpose" in the search for the correct form of the rule of law. To the courts, "integrity of purpose" forms the basis of a legal principle – the principle of legality – that allows them to declare Acts of Parliament unconstitutional, and also to correct unlawful (in a rather broad sense) executive acts by way of judicial review. Every law enacted by Parliament has a purpose, to achieve a desired end or outcome. The rule of law requires that the law be enforced for that purpose and not for any other purpose outside the scope of the legislation, i.e. an "extraneous purpose" in judicial language. An extraneous purpose need not necessarily be an evil purpose, but it is still an unauthorised purpose. The law rules, but only to the extent to which unlawful acts have been done. For the law to do otherwise would be contrary to the rule of law – a misuse of the law, resulting in the misrule of law. Hence, political opponents, dissidents and critics who criticise the government, however persistently or vehemently, for its policies or performance or on any issue of public interest, are not under any risk of being detained lawfully under the ISA as such criticisms do not affect national security.

## FREEDOM OF SPEECH –
## DEFAMATION AND CONTEMPT OF COURT

The other criticism concerns defamation and contempt of court. Critics have claimed or alleged that ministers have used the law of defamation to stifle freedom of expression. This argument is premised on the principle that it is somehow wrong for ministers to sue people who violate their right to reputation. In every democratic society, freedom of speech has to be balanced against other competing interests. Each society sets its own balance to reflect its own values. In Singapore, the Constitution has settled the balance in favour of, *inter alia*, public order, personal reputation and the authority of the courts.[22] Why should ministers and the courts be barred from defending or vindicating their rights by an open and transparent process? There is room in the marketplace of ideas for the expression of opinions – controversial or offensive views or bad ideas – but why should defamatory speech that harms the victim's reputation be accorded free reign?

Defamatory speech is by definition speech which is false and which injures the reputation of the victim. False statements concerning the character of a person, be he a minister or any other member of the community, have no social, political or scientific value which justifies protection by the law. No truth of any kind that may benefit society can come out of a false statement except the truth of its falsity. But truth is a defence and so is fair comment if there is a factual basis upon which the comments were made without malice and in the public interest. As for contempt of court, there is also no social value in making false statements that undermine (or which may have a tendency to undermine) the authority of the courts or public confidence in the courts. Courts give reasons for their decisions which are subject to public scrutiny and comment. False statements are also defamatory of the judiciary which is an indispensable institution in upholding the rule of law.

*Chan Sek Keong*

65

## CONCLUDING OBSERVATIONS

Foreign criticisms of Mr Lee's rule of law are based on ideological principles to which Mr Lee does not subscribe, and which have only peripheral bearing on the rule of law. Ideologies are intellectual constructs based on abstract reasoning based on *a priori* principles which may not necessarily reflect the realities of concrete situations, such as the circumstances of societies at various stages of social and economic development. Moreover, they cannot possibly reflect the complexities of the human psyche and human behaviour which have evolved differently in different societies over many millennia of civilisation.

A leading rule of law scholar wrote in 2012:

> [T]here... *is no one manifestation* of the rule of law. There are many different ways and textures to how countries manifest the rule of law... The rule of law in Japan is very different from the rule of law in Germany, which is different from the rule of law in Singapore and in the United States. All these societies have recognisably robust rule of law systems, albeit with different strengths and weaknesses. And within each society, the implications of their rule of law system – how it plays out in daily life – is a function of the surrounding political, economic, cultural and social environment.
>
> What this insight tells us is that ... what really matters is the role rule of law plays within the broader government and society on issues of importance to the people, whether the legal system on the whole, or in the particular instances, is a positive force for good, or not.[23]

These views are consonant with Mr Lee's approach to the rule of law.

Hence foreign criticisms of Mr Lee's rule of law are misplaced. Mr Lee's rule of law has contributed to making Singapore what it is today – an oasis of peace, stability and prosperity in an uncertain, turbulent and violent world. Singapore is lucky to have as its first prime minister a brilliant lawyer who understands the uses, power and limits of the law to change society for the better, and who has made full use of the rule of law, in the words of the Proclamation of Independence, to purposefully seek "the welfare and happiness of her people in a more just and equal society".[24]

## Endnotes

1 See FA Hayek, *The Constitution of Liberty* (London: Routledge & Kegan Paul, 1960), p. 165, citing Aristotle's *Politics* in footnote 25.

2 Ibid., p. 166.

3 For a short account of the influence of the Magna Carta 1215 on the development of the rule of law in England, see Tom Bingham, *The Rule of Law* (London: Allen Lane, 2010, pp. 10–13) ("*Bingham*").

4 See *Bingham*, p. 12.

5 See *Bingham*, pp. 3–5 for an elaboration of these meanings.

6 See "The Rule of Law and Human Rights – Principles and Definitions" (The International Commission of Jurists, Geneva 1966) which contains the texts of the Universal Declaration of Human Rights 1948 and the declarations made at assemblies and forums by judges, lawyers and jurists organised by the International Commission of Jurists in the Act of Athens 1955, the Declaration of Delhi 1959, and the Law of Lagos 1961.

**7** See Thomas Carothers, *Rule-of-Law Revival* (1998) and *Rule of Law Temptations* (2009).

**8** Professor Brian Tamanaha, "The History and Elements of the Rule of Law", *Singapore Journal of Legal Studies*, 2012, p. 232.

**9** Lee Kuan Yew, press conference with the Singapore media in Beijing, 12 June 2001. *The Papers of Lee Kuan Yew: Speeches, Interviews and Dialogues, vol. 17: 2006–2008* (Singapore: Gale Asia, 2013), p. 134.

**10** In 1948, an "Emergency" (rather than a declaration of war) was declared in Malaya following the Communist Party of Malaya's decision to engage in armed conflict with the British for control of Malaya. A set of draconian laws known as the Emergency Regulations was issued in 1948 which permitted detention without trial. These regulations were not an innovation but based on DORA. The Emergency was still on in 1957 when the British granted full independence to the Malay States, Penang and Malacca on 31 August 1957 as the Federation of Malaya. The Federation adopted a constitution (the 1957 Malayan Constitution) based on the Westminster model, i.e. a parliamentary form of government based on the principles of the United Kingdom's unwritten constitution. The structure of government was based on the separation of powers, with the legislature, the executive and the judiciary sharing constitutional power as co-equals, each within its sphere of constitutional power. The 1957 Malayan Constitution also incorporated in Part II certain fundamental liberties such as liberty of the person, rights, subject to specific qualifications (i.e. a qualified bill of rights) in Part II. It also contained a provision, Article 4, which declared its supremacy over all other laws. Hence, unlike the UK Parliament, the Malayan Parliament was not sovereign. The 1948 Emergency Regulations continued in force as a qualification to the fundamental liberties granted by the 1957 Constitution.

**11** Reproduced in full in Han Fook Kwang, Warren Fernandez, Sumiko Tan, *Lee Kuan Yew: The Man and His Ideas* (Singapore: Times Editions, 1998), p. 411.

**12** Michael Barr, *Lee Kuan Yew – The Beliefs behind the Man* (Kuala Lumpur: New Asian Library, 2009), p. 61.

**13** Lee Kuan Yew, 28 March 2001 interview with Tom Plate. *The Papers of Lee Kuan Yew: Speeches, Interviews and Dialogues, vol. 17: 2006–2008* (Singapore: Gale Asia, 2013), p. 14.

**14** Joseph Raz, "The Rule of Law and its Virtue", *Law Quarterly Review* (1977), pp. 195–211, at p. 196.

**15** Lawyers' Rights Watch Canada, *Rule of Law in Singapore: Independence of the Judiciary and the Legal Profession in Singapore* (Vancouver: LRWC), 2007. See also Chan Sek Keong, "The Courts and the Rule of Law in Singapore", *Singapore Journal of Legal Studies*, 2012, pp. 209–231.

**16** See app.subcourts.gov.sg/.../Speeches/2007Oct14_IBA_MMLeeKeynote.pd.

**17** International Bar Association Human Rights Institute, "Prosperity Versus Individual Rights?: Human Rights, Democracy and the Rule of Law in Singapore" (London: International Bar Association, 2008).

**18** During a dialogue session at the Russia-Singapore Business Forum held on 6 March 2007, Mr Lee said, "I do not subscribe to the American liberal theory that democracy and the free market will solve everything. I believe you've got to have order, discipline, rule of law, certainty of daily life and you must make work, learning, studying rewarding. If you can make money by cheating, by robbing, by stealing, nobody is going to spend time learning how to make machine tools or how to plan a building or whatever. From my experience, that was what we went through when the Japanese occupied Singapore." *The Papers of Lee Kuan Yew: Speeches, Interviews and Dialogues, vol. 17: 2006-2008* (Singapore: Gale Asia, 2013), pp. 195-209, at p. 199.

**19** At a doorstop interview at the Australian National University in Canberra, Australia on 28 March 2007, the interviewer asked Mr Lee, "The point the protestors were making was human rights violations in Singapore and the rule of law in Singapore, the quieting of dissent in Singapore. How do you respond to that, Sir?" Mr Lee responded, "I go by the rules of governance. You measure us on every single yardstick of governance and you find, look up the *World Economic Forum Global Competitiveness Report* and you run through every single item – rule of law, transparency, integrity of the system, efficiency of the civil service, confidence of the courts, both domestically and internationally – Singapore is at the top." *The Papers of Lee Kuan Yew: Speeches, Interviews and Dialogues, vol. 17: 2006-2008* (Singapore: Gale Asia, 2013), p. 216.

**20** See Chan Sek Keong, "The Courts and the Rule of Law in Singapore", *Singapore Journal of Legal Studies*, 2012, p. 209. Another example would be of a case where a detention order is made against the detainee's lawyer on the basis that his legal advice or representation in court is determined by the President to be prejudicial to the security of Singapore: see the Court of Appeal's observations in *Teo Soh Lung v Minister for Home Affairs* [1990] 1 SLR (R) 347 (CA) at paras 34, 35 and 41.

**21** Article 9(1) of the Constitution provides: "No person shall be deprived of his life or personal liberty save in accordance with law".

**22** Article 14 provides:
Freedom of speech
14. (1) Subject to clause (2) (a) every citizen of Singapore has the right to freedom of speech and expression;
(2) Parliament may by law impose on the rights conferred by clause (1)(a), such restrictions as it considers necessary or expedient in the interest of the security of Singapore or any part thereof, friendly relations with other countries, public order or morality and restrictions designed to protect the privileges of Parliament or to provide against contempt of court, defamation or incitement to any offence.

**23** Tamanaha, "The History", p. 247.

**24** On 9 August 1965, Lee Kuan Yew proclaimed Singapore's independence and sovereignty, separately from Malaysia's legislative act to allow Singapore to leave the Federation of Malaysia.

# ORDER AND LAW?
# LEE KUAN YEW AND THE RULE OF LAW

———

*S Jayakumar*

LEE KUAN YEW'S speeches contain such a wealth of material on his approach to law, the legal system, and order and security that they could easily form the basis of a thesis for any budding doctoral student. There are also good accounts already published, most notably *Lee Kuan Yew: The Man and His Ideas* by Han Fook Kwang, Warren Fernandez and Sumiko Tan.

Given this wealth of materials, and the constraints of space, it is not possible for me to give a comprehensive or a learned analysis. Instead, I propose to share with you some of my takeaways and lessons, as well as some personal stories and reflections after many years of working closely with Mr Lee on matters relating to the legal system, the rule of law and issues of order and security.

I worked with him in many capacities during the time I was minister for home affairs (1984–1994), minister for foreign affairs (1994–2004) and also minister for law (1988–2008).

## BASIC APPROACH TO LAW

Mr Lee never viewed law and the legal system in isolation. To him, law and the legal system were an integral part of his overall vision and strategy to shape Singapore's future. His starting point was: what will serve Singapore's national interest best? From there, work out the correct policy options.

His single-minded goal was to ensure that Singapore would succeed. Law was an instrument to give effect to his overall strategy and vision for the country. If new laws were needed or if laws had to be amended, his attitude was: get it done to ensure that policy is effectively implemented. He was not averse to trying out novel and unusual legal solutions. This is because Singapore's situation and circumstances were unusual.

He always reminded us: Singapore is not an "ordinary" country. We are tiny, with no natural resources, and one of the most densely populated countries in the world. Since our society is multiracial and multi-religious, the potential for disorder and racial discord is high. Also, Singapore is situated in a turbulent region with two large neighbours, each of which had quarters resentful and envious of our independence.

This approach was pervasive and covered all fields. For example: (a) to ensure housing estates were quickly built we passed the Land Acquisition laws, which favoured the State on compensation to be paid; (b) to ensure law and order we enacted "tough laws" in areas of corruption, drugs and vandalism. "Tough" penalties like caning and the death penalty were implemented too.

## MAKING SINGAPORE AN "OASIS"

There are many references in Mr Lee's speeches, from 1960s onwards, about making Singapore a First World oasis in a Third World region. However, his idea of an oasis was not just making this "one of the cleanest and most beautiful cities in Asia, with trees, flowers and shrubs in all the public places"[1] nor was it just about excellent infrastructure (roads, airports, seaports, communications, health or schooling).[2]

Yes, all those aspects were important to him, but his concept of "oasis" also clearly included law, order and security.

> To attract foreign investment to Singapore, our strategy was to make Singapore a First World oasis in a Third World region at the time. We had to distinguish ourselves from our neighbours by being more stable and secure, with a sound legal system and the rule of law, impartially administered...[3]
>
> We set out to become an oasis where First World standards are maintained, not just the infrastructure but services for corporations and people, the security and certainty, the predictability... Plus personal security, low crime rate; you can go jogging at two o'clock in the morning and feel safe.[4]

72

He grasped something that many other newly independent countries had not appreciated – that unless there is respect for the rule of law and there is a sense of safety and security, Singapore will not obtain investments, tourists and the confidence of its own people.

## APPROACH TO COMMERCIAL LAW

Lee Kuan Yew's key aim was to ensure stability, safety, security and the absence of corruption. All these elements were essential for economic growth and investor confidence.

Right from independence, he realised the importance of the rule of law for the stability of the country. To this end, Mr Lee will stand by unpopular decisions. For example, to ensure the quality of the civil service and to remove the temptation of corruption, he has always strongly advocated competitive salaries for civil servants.

These efforts were vindicated when Singapore was recognised by independent rating agencies including Political and Economic Risk Consultancy, World Economic Forum, International Institute for Management Development and Transparency International, to uphold the rule of law, to have an independent and capable judiciary, to maintain high standards of transparency and to not tolerate corruption. He successfully drew in investments from all the developed economies and made Singapore one of the leading banking and financial services hubs in Asia.[5] As he later observed:

> Our reputation for the rule of law has been and is a valuable economic asset, part of our capital, although an intangible one... A country that has no rule of law, where the government acts capriciously, is not a country wealthy men from other countries would sink money in real estate.[6]

Mr Lee had studied law at Cambridge and was a barrister of the Middle Temple. He had practised law for a decade before becoming prime minister. He attributed these factors to his knowledge "that the rule of law would give Singapore an advantage in the centre of Southeast Asia".[7]

His British education and exposure influenced his view of fair play, which is why he retained judicial review, ensuring that public bodies with statutory powers behaved legally and fairly.

Although he was British-trained, he never hesitated to learn from other jurisdictions. But ultimately he would choose to go by what would work best for Singapore in the context of our unique circumstances. His starting point was to adopt and preserve the laws that we had inherited, whether from

Britain, India or Malaysia – because they were tried and tested, were sound and intellectually robust – and then to make changes to fit our circumstances. When Section 5 of the Civil Law Act created uncertainty on the continuing reception of English commercial law, Mr Lee addressed it by enacting the Application of English Law Act, under the recommendation of then High Court judge, Chan Sek Keong.

On commercial and banking laws, he would insist on checking which other countries have had the same issues and as far as possible follow their models. In this area, he would prefer that we look towards the established UK, US and European models. He had good reasons for this: he wanted Singapore to succeed as a commercial and financial centre. To achieve that, foreign investors must have confidence in our laws, our legal system, and in the independence and impartiality of our judiciary. They would have confidence and comfort if the legal norms were those they were familiar with.

He would always advise the Attorney General's Chambers not to re-invent the wheel. Whenever faced with a problem, his approach was to check how reputable jurisdictions – primarily the UK and US – have tackled the problem; examine their models, and if suitable adapt them for our purpose. However, he would not hesitate to try novel approaches – for example, in the area of Land Acquisition Laws and Singapore's En Bloc System.

Mr Lee also played a pivotal role in liberalising the legal profession in Singapore. Through a calibrated move, foreign competition was introduced in order to raise the bar for local firms and to provide foreign investors with greater choice of legal representation. This strengthened the quality and range of legal services while attracting foreign investments. Today, Singapore's legal sector is easily one of the most liberalised in the region.

Singapore law firms have also grown both domestically and regionally through this initiative.

## APPROACH TO ORDER AND SECURITY

To Mr Lee, establishment of order was the priority. As he explained to an audience of law students in 1962:

> Those of you who are just embarking on the study of the law will learn the phrase "law and order". In a settled and established society, law appears to be a precursor of order. Good laws lead to good order – that is the form that you will learn. But the hard realities of keeping the peace between man and man, and between authority and the individual can be more accurately described if the phrase were inverted to "order and law", for without order, the operation of law is impossible. Order having been established and the rules having become enforceable in a settled society, only then is it possible to work out human relationships between subject and subject, and subject and the state in accordance with predetermined rules of law.[8]

The Rule of Law is about the balance between the rights of individuals and the interests of the society. In this equation, Mr Lee would clearly tilt the balance in favour of overall societal interests:[9]

> The basic difference in our approach springs from our traditional Asian value system which places interests of the community over and above that of the individual. In English doctrine, the rights of the individual must be the paramount consideration. We shook ourselves free from

the confines of English norms which did not accord with the customs and values of Singapore society. In criminal law legislation, our priority is the security and well-being of law-abiding citizens rather than the rights of the criminal to be protected from incriminating evidence.[10]

Mr Lee's priority was to ensure that people, Singaporeans and foreigners alike, felt safe and secure in this densely populated city. His belief was that the natural order of things is disorder. So, it was imperative to establish a framework of law and order:

> Human beings in a lumpen mass, whether they be in a refugee camp or in a refugee boat, are just so many individuals seeking individual or family survival; often, they become anarchic. It is only when there is the social framework of law and order, with the police to enforce the law, the courts to mete out punishment or settle disputes, the schools to educate and train children, doctors and hospitals to care for the sick and work to bring money rewards with which to buy one's needs, only then can a society enable the individual to flourish and flower.[11]

76

He advocated tough deterrent laws and penalties with respect to vandalism, guns, drugs and kidnapping even though we came in for criticisms from various Western quarters.

Mr Lee would never be apologetic about our system and our approach. His approach was: we will do what works best for Singapore and robustly defend our approach. This was evident when he rebutted foreign critics in the Michael Fay episode, an incident that should be familiar to all.

## RACE, RELIGION AND THE RULE OF LAW

Other essays in this volume speak about Mr Lee's concern for racial and religious harmony. What I wish to highlight is that to him it was also a key component of the rule of law, and a key aspect of his oasis vision. Singapore would be different from other countries, many of which were plagued by tensions and conflict due to issues of race, religion and language.

There are two aspects of this vision. First, that the laws and Constitution should provide for non-discrimination:

> I want to add to this Constitution certain safeguards which will make it necessary, whatever party comes into power, to honour and respect minority rights. This is a multiracial nation. This is not a Malay nation which some people tried to make it and this is not a Chinese nation.[12]

In order to formulate constitutional safeguards of non-discrimination, the Wee Chong Jin Constitutional Commission 1966 was appointed. I also worked with Mr Lee on the Maintenance of Religious Harmony Act (1989) which allows the government to effectively deal with situations that threaten religious harmony in Singapore.

The second aspect was his consistent, tough approach with anyone who sought to stir up racial or religious trouble. When I was minister for home affairs, his advice was to always nip things in the bud:

> I give you my assurance that anybody whether he is Chinese, Indian, Malay or Eurasian or any other race, whoever starts trouble we smack him down. And the police and the army will carry out the orders in a disciplined and fair way.[13]

It went beyond laws and law enforcement – he would always remind the Cabinet of the importance of Singapore being a multiracial society. I recall him noticing that on one Singapore Airlines flight that he had flown, the cabin crew had no Malay, Indian or Eurasian members. Upon his return, he asked the minister for transport to give feedback to Singapore Airlines: international passengers should not think that Singapore was just a Chinese nation.

As a citizen as well as a member of the Indian minority community, I feel strongly that his philosophy and approach gave minorities equal opportunities and dignity. This was not just lip service – he practised what he preached. I think one of his greatest contributions was to ensure that racial harmony became part of Singapore's DNA and that DNA is embedded in the rule of law in Singapore.

## APPROACH TO THE CONSTITUTIONAL DEVELOPMENT

For many years after Separation, Mr Lee was quite content to have a rather inelegant, untidy constitutional arrangement. We did not have one single comprehensive new constitution; instead we had the old constitution meant for a constituent state within Malaysia, together with certain provisions of the Malaysian federal constitution deemed to be applicable, and we also had the Republic of Singapore Independence Act. He conceded that "In 1970, our Constitution was in a mess – part state constitution, part federal, part amendments after Separation. Untidy."[14]

However, he decided to leave the Constitution as it was, to just incorporate all the amendments and publish a clean copy. He explained that his decision was based on real-life learning and hands-on experience, and from watching the Malaysian constitution being amended over a hundred times in just under three years since it had been promulgated (and it has gone through many more since then).[15]

He gave an interesting analogy which explained this cautious approach:

From my experience, constitutions have to be custom-made, tailored to suit the peculiarities of the person wearing the suit. Perhaps, like shoes, the older they are, the better they fit. Stretch them, soften them, resole them, repair them. They are always better than a brand new pair of shoes...

...I believe it is better to stretch and ease an old shoe when we know that the different shape and fit of a younger generation requires a change. It is a change to meet the future.[16]

He elaborated that many other post-colonial countries had tried and gone through several constitutions since independence: from parliamentary to presidential government, on to military rule, back to elections for a president, on to a people's republic, back to a revolutionary junta. These constitutions had brought neither stability nor legitimacy.

Nonetheless, even in the area of constitutional law, he did not hesitate pushing for novel approaches. Three examples come to mind: First, the Westminster parliamentary system was amended to incorporate an Elected President with custodial powers over the reserves and key appointments in Parliament. Second, the Group Representation Constituency (GRC) scheme was implemented so as to ensure minority representation in Parliament and prevent voting along racial lines. Third, the Non-Constituency Members of Parliament (NCMP) scheme was implemented so as to ensure that opposition voices would be heard in Parliament.

## RULE OF LAW IN INTERNATIONAL RELATIONS

Mr Lee's approach to law in international relations has mirrored his approach to the role of law within a State. His view is that observance of international law is important for all nations, but critically important for small countries like Singapore.

There are many examples to illustrate this, such as our relations with Malaysia on the Water Agreements, or his strong stand against Vietnam's use of force in Cambodia. He felt it important that Singapore observed international law, and that we observed agreements. On the flip side, he wanted other countries to honour agreements with us. If we had disputes, then he favoured third party adjudication when negotiations led to an impasse. A good example is the Pedra Branca case with Malaysia.

## LEE KUAN YEW'S STYLE AND APPROACH

Let me now move on to discuss some common myths about Lee Kuan Yew's style and approach. The first myth is that he is dictatorial; he insists on getting his way in Cabinet.

Yes, he has strong views, but he is willing to be persuaded by cogent, contrary views. For example, with regard to the proposal on the Elected President, contrary to popular perception, Lee Kuan Yew was not a dictatorial prime minister who railroaded his proposals through a meek, spineless Cabinet. Instead, Mr Lee took a collegiate approach. He wanted an Elected President scheme which younger ministers could live with. He allowed a vigorous debate between ministers on the proposals and he participated in them. As the deliberations went on, he told ministers that it was worth taking our time to carefully consider the proposals. Ultimately, while he responded fully to criticisms of his proposals from Cabinet colleagues,

Mr Lee was prepared to be persuaded to modify his position and accept the views of the younger ministers.

It is true that he can be impatient: once he embarks on a particular course of action, he wants it seen through without delay. However, I always found him to be intellectually honest. When a persuasive, cogent argument is made for an alternative policy or decision, he would be prepared to listen, reflect on it, and even modify his original proposal.

The second myth is that he was quick to institute defamation actions because he was confident that the judges would always rule in his favour. From my own experience working with Mr Lee, I believe he took the independence and impartiality of the judges very seriously. I once sat in discussions with Queen's Counsels (QCs) when he took the libel action against the *Far Eastern Economic Review* in 1987. He spent much time brainstorming with the QCs, and wanted to be very sure that he had a very good case. As one senior counsel who has worked closely with him told me:

> I found that he took no chances, suggesting both that he never believed the courts were partial to him and that he had to be 100 per cent sure he would win on the law before taking action. In none of the cases that I did for him did he act in a way contrary to my advice or the advice of the QC. If I said that his case was unclear, he would not sue or would ask me to take the QC's opinion. Unless the QC advises that he has a strong case, he would not sue.
>
> This not only showed that he followed legal advice; more importantly, he was sending the message that if he wins, then just like all successful parties, he wins on the law and on the merits of the case.[17]

*S Jayakumar*

81

## MAIN TAKEAWAYS

Younger lawyers often ask me what my main takeaways are from having worked with Mr Lee. Two aspects of the man have had a lasting impact on me.

First, he stood up firmly for what he believed. Singapore had unusual circumstances and the solutions and approach he adopted came in for criticisms, especially from the West. One important lesson he taught me was to always work out what suits our national interests best, and once you have decided, never be afraid to defend it. His approach was: whatever you do or say, be prepared to defend it robustly.

This was exemplified in the way Mr Lee handled the Bernard Levin incident in the 1990s. The British journalist Bernard Levin wrote critical pieces in the UK press attacking Singapore and Mr Lee. There was one especially vitriolic piece he wrote in *The Times*, in April 1990. Mr Lee was scheduled to visit London then and he wrote to the editor of *The Times* proposing that instead of a unilateral reply by him to *The Times*, there should be a no-holds-barred TV interview on the BBC, where he could be fully questioned by Levin. *The Times* editor replied that he doubted if any TV channel would be interested in giving such airtime. But Mr Lee had written to the chairman of the BBC who was taken with the idea and agreed. However, Levin later balked, and there was no debate, but instead the BBC itself did an interview with Mr Lee.

Mr Lee then asked me to work with our Mission in London to take out full-page paid advertisements in other UK newspapers to set out the full facts and expose how he had proposed a face-to-face interview, and that Levin had declined. We wondered if they would agree, or if they would show solidarity with *The Times*. Mr Lee was quite sure that they would not pass up the chance to make money. That is exactly what happened –

*The Independent* published the full-page advertisement and other newspapers also ran stories about it!

Secondly, I was impressed by his thoroughness in preparation. He would leave no stone unturned when considering any problem, legal or otherwise. This can be illustrated by the Bernard Levin episode again. Mr Lee was about to leave for London after he had proposed the debate with Levin. We did not know if the debate would actually take place. Nonetheless, he was preparing for it carefully. Before he left for London, he phoned me at home and said he wanted to brainstorm the issues. I said of course, but asked, when was he leaving? He said the following night. His schedule was tight for that day. He then in a very polite way asked if it would be convenient for me to come over to his house. It was past 10 pm, and I said sure. I went over to his Oxley Road home, and we chatted in his room on the lower floor. He asked me to go over the most difficult questions and criticisms that could be levelled at him and Singapore. He would then go over how he proposed to reply, and what I thought of it, and this went on till near midnight until he seemed satisfied that we had gone over all possible issues. I was struck by the sheer thoroughness of his preparation.

I hope what I have said so far makes it clear that Lee Kuan Yew's approach to the rule of law has been a major factor in Singapore's success. Let me close by saying that I have worked with subsequent prime minsters, Goh Chok Tong and Lee Hsien Loong. They are not lawyers, but what cheers me about Singapore's future is that these leaders and their Cabinet colleagues have instinctively understood the importance of maintaining the basic approaches to the rule of law espoused by Mr Lee. Of course under their charge, laws will evolve with the changing times, but the basic and fundamental features of Mr Lee's approach to the law have become firmly ingrained.

*S Jayakumar*

83

## Endnotes

**1** Lee Kuan Yew, "National Service to Be Introduced: Speech at the Ceremony of Conferment of the Public Service Star Awards on Tan Tong Meng and Inche Buang B. Siraj, Toa Payoh Community Centre (21 February 1967)". *The Papers of Lee Kuan Yew: Speeches, Interviews and Dialogues, vol. 4: 1967–1968* (Singapore: Gale Asia, 2012), p. 33.

**2** "First Interview with Yoshinori Imai, Nippon Hoso Kyokai at the Istana, Singapore (18 December 1999)". *The Papers of Lee Kuan Yew: Speeches, Interviews and Dialogues, vol. 14: 1999–2000* (Singapore: Gale Asia, 2013), p. 127.

**3** Lee Kuan Yew, "The Role of Singapore in the Asian Boom: Speech at the International Graduate School of Management in Barcelona, Spain (13 September 2005)". *The Papers of Lee Kuan Yew: Speeches, Interviews and Dialogues, vol. 16: 2004–2006* (Singapore: Gale Asia, 2013), p. 410.

**4** "Interview with Michael Bociurkiw, the *Forbes* Magazine at the Istana, Singapore (3 August 2001)". *The Papers of Lee Kuan Yew: Speeches, Interviews and Dialogues, vol. 15: 2001–2003* (Singapore: Gale Asia, 2013), p. 152.

**5** See also Lee Kuan Yew, "The Legal Fundamentals on which Singapore is Built: Speech at the Opening of the International Bar Association Conference at the Suntec Singapore International Convention & Exhibition Centre, Singapore (14 October 2007)". *The Papers of Lee Kuan Yew: Speeches, Interviews and Dialogues, vol. 17: 2006–2008* (Singapore: Gale Asia, 2013), p. 463, where he said, "To survive we had to create a Singapore different from our neighbours – clean, more efficient, more secure… Important for investors and economic growth is the rule of law implemented through an independent judiciary, an honest and efficient police force, and effective law enforcement agencies. Had we not differentiated Singapore in this way, it would have languished and perished as a shrinking trading centre instead of becoming the thriving, banking, shipping and aviation hub it is today."

**6** *Singapore Parliamentary Debates, Official Report*, 2 November 1995, vol. 65 at col. 236 (Lee Kuan Yew, Senior Minister).

**7** Lee Kuan Yew, "The Legal Fundamentals on which Singapore is Built: Speech at the Opening of the International Bar Association Conference at the Suntec Singapore International Convention & Exhibition Centre, Singapore (14 October 2007)". *The Papers of Lee Kuan Yew: Speeches, Interviews and Dialogues, vol. 17: 2006-2008* (Singapore: Gale Asia, 2013), p. 463.

**8** Lee Kuan Yew, "Law and Order, Justice and Fair Play: Speech at the University of Singapore Law Society's Annual Dinner at Rosee d'Or (18 January 1962)". *The Papers of Lee Kuan Yew: Speeches, Interviews and Dialogues, vol. 1: 1950-1962* (Singapore: Gale Asia, 2012), p. 323.

**9** On another occasion, he said: "The expansion of the right of the individual to behave or misbehave as he pleases has come at the expense of orderly society. In the East the main object is to have a well-ordered society so that everybody can have maximum enjoyment of his freedoms. This freedom can only exist in an ordered state and not in a natural state of contention and anarchy." See Fareed Zakaria, "Culture Is Destiny: A Conversation with Lee Kuan Yew", *Foreign Affairs*, March/April 1994, vol. 3, Issue 2, p. 111.

**10** Lee Kuan Yew, "Law as Expressions of Philosophy of Government: Speech delivered at the Opening of the Academy of Law (31 August 1990)". *The Papers of Lee Kuan Yew: Speeches, Interviews and Dialogues, vol. 10: 1988-1990* (Singapore: Gale Asia, 2012), pp. 661-662.

**11** Lee Kuan Yew, "Changing Our Habits to Improve the Language Environment: Speech at the *Chap Goh Mei* Party at the Istana, Singapore (11 February 1979)". *The Papers of Lee Kuan Yew: Speeches, Interviews and Dialogues, vol. 8: 1978-1980* (Singapore: Gale Asia, 2012), p. 284.

**12** Lee Kuan Yew, "*Au Revoir* to Malaysia: Press Conference at Cabinet Office, City Hall, after the Meeting of Singaporean and Malaysian People's Action Party Leaders (12 August 1965)". *The Papers of Lee Kuan Yew: Speeches, Interviews and Dialogues, vol. 3: 1965-1966* (Singapore: Gale Asia, 2012), p. 34.

**13** Lee Kuan Yew, "Speech at the Potong Pasir PAP Branch (31 May 1969)". *The Papers of Lee Kuan Yew: Speeches, Interviews and Dialogues, vol. 5: 1969-1971* (Singapore: Gale Asia, 2012), p. 110.

**14** *Singapore Parliamentary Debates*, Official Report (25 July 1984), vol. 44 at col. 1818 (Lee Kuan Yew, Prime Minister).

**15** *Singapore Parliamentary Debates*, Official Report (25 July 1984), vol. 44 at cols. 1807-1832 (Lee Kuan Yew, Prime Minister).

**16** *Singapore Parliamentary Debates*, Official Report (24 July 1984), vol. 44 at cols. 1735-1736 (Lee Kuan Yew, Prime Minister).

**17** Private communication

PART
3

# GOVERNANCE

## Reasonable Men Adapt, Unreasonable Men Change the World

Peter Ho

## The Making of the Singapore Public Service

*Yong Ying-I*

# REASONABLE MEN ADAPT, UNREASONABLE MEN CHANGE THE WORLD

*Peter Ho*

WHEN I WAS much younger, I was called up to the Istana one afternoon along with a few other officers for a discussion on a paper that we had written. Lee Kuan Yew, then prime minister, gently chastised us for the paper, which he said was good, but only in a theoretical way. He was a practical person, so he expected assessments and recommendations to be practical, reflecting the real world.

Then, his mood mellowed. He started talking more generally about the challenges facing Singapore. He said something that is indelibly imprinted  in my memory: "Reasonable men adapt, unreasonable men change the world." Of course, he left us in no doubt as to which category he belonged. By the way, I later discovered that this remark paraphrased a quote from George Bernard Shaw.

When I think of Lee Kuan Yew and his impact on governance in Singapore, I am reminded of what he said to us that afternoon many years ago. Above all, the government that he led for so many years, and the outcomes that he created for Singapore, were acts of political will and leadership.

As prime minister, Mr Lee set the tone, the pace and the direction for government. As civil servants, we took our cues from him, not just because of his position but also because of his character, his intellectual strength and his sense of purpose. He seemed to us like a force of nature. He was the leader of the pack, the alpha male, and we counted ourselves fortunate to have someone like him in charge. When things seemed most difficult, he showed us the way forward. Whether such moments were just acts of bravado, or evidence of great foresight, I guess only he will know. But he inspired confidence. By word and deed, and by his personal actions, he forged a spirit, an ethos and an attitude in the Singapore Public Service that is the foundation of our approach to governance that has sustained us to this day.

*Peter Ho*

## POLITICAL WILL

Singapore has been called the improbable nation. Lee Kuan Yew, when announcing separation from Malaysia, said that it was "a moment of anguish because all my life... I have believed in Malaysian merger and the unity of the two territories".[1]

But he had to make independence work. "I had first to demonstrate that Singapore could survive without living off the economies of Indonesia and Malaysia. We were not parasites dependent only on our neighbours."[2]

His character is tough, even bloody-minded, as the British would put it. In describing Mr Lee to then British Prime Minister Harold MacMillan, Duncan Sandys, the minister at the Commonwealth Relations Office, said that he "is not a man who climbs down. Once he has committed himself to a definite course and has accepted a carefully calculated risk, he is likely to go through with it, for better or worse ..."[3]

Indeed, Mr Lee has described himself as "very determined". He has said, "If I decide that something is worth doing, then I'll put my heart and soul to it. I'll give everything I've got to make it succeed. So I would put my strength, determination and willingness to see my objective to its conclusion."[4]

We in the civil service learnt from him that having reached a decision, one had to stay the course. Indeed, I would argue that strong will was the key that propelled Singapore from a Third World backwater into the First World in less than two generations.

## PRAGMATIC GOVERNANCE, PRACTICAL GOVERNMENT

Lee Kuan Yew describes himself as a pragmatist. According to him, "we – Dr Goh Keng Swee, myself, Hon Sui Sen, Lim Kim San – we were the pragmatists".[5] He argued that "as the world changes, small countries have to swiftly adjust their policies and positions in a pragmatic and clinical manner. We have to live with the world as it is, not as we wish it should be. We must remain nimble to seize opportunities that come with changing circumstances, or to get out of harm's way."[6]

Reflecting this pragmatism, the government chose foreign direct investment – in the form of attracting MNCs to Singapore – over the prevailing dogma of the day, which viewed MNCs as a form of neo-colonialism. For Mr Lee, it was about creating jobs for the people, not political correctness. These outcomes are the ends that justify the means.

This approach has shaped the government's thinking and policies. Ideology is eschewed. The focus is on outcomes and results.

## EXPERIMENTATION AND INNOVATION

The pragmatic approach has clearly made a difference. But while necessary, it is not always sufficient. Looking back, many of the early policies of the Lee Kuan Yew government had no precedent.

Housing, the development of Jurong Industrial Estate, foreign direct investment – any one of them could have failed, instead of going on to be success stories. Mr Lee said as much, admitting that "so many other things could go wrong, you know. But we could safeguard ourselves against these if we remember that there are certain ideals, certain standards, certain norms which are desirable and should be striven for; then relate those to your existing society, your existing circumstances: what is achievable in this given situation. The crucial thing is: do not be afraid to innovate."[7]

Mr Lee recounted how Hon Sui Sen came to see him with a bold idea on the Asian Dollar Market obtained from a Dutch manager of the Bank of America in Singapore, Van Oenen. Hon Sui Sen said: "Let's take a chance. Change our foreign exchange regulations. Release it." Hon Sui Sen also said, with regard to foreign exchange controls: "Cancel it. Let's start the Asian Currency Unit. Collect all the dollars in the region, lend it to the world. We will be the link between New York closing and London opening." Mr Lee listened intently and then told Hon Sui Sen: "Proceed."[8]

This spirit clearly guides the government. It is a myth that everything in Singapore is planned down to the $n^{th}$ degree, that nothing is expected to go wrong and that the government operates in a fail-safe mode. Many big leaps forward have been nothing more than acts of faith. The first container port at Tanjong Pagar was a big risk, as the container was by no means a proven mode of transportation. But Mr Lee gave Howe Yoon Chong, who was then chairman of the Port of Singapore Authority (PSA), enough leeway to make the move to Tanjong Pagar.

Of course, it is not about taking reckless risks. Many of these projects could have been stillborn if not for hard work and persistence. I recall Howe Yoon Chong telling me that he failed repeatedly to persuade the PSA Board to build the container port. Then he brought in consultants, at great cost. Their analysis eventually persuaded the Board that the container port was the right way to go. In Howe Yoon Chong's view, the cost of the consultancy was money well spent.

That willingness to try things out spawned a generation of state entrepreneurs who created, almost out of nothing, national icons such as Singapore Airlines, DBS, ST Engineering, Changi Airport, SingTel and so on. The national computerisation programme, started in the Ministry of Defence, is another example of a policy that transformed Singapore.

## BUT NO SHORT CUTS

But there are no short cuts, and "cowboys" are not tolerated in government. As civil servants, we were constantly amazed by Mr Lee's breadth and depth. On anything that matters to him, and to Singapore, he has a considered view. So it meant that we had to be as sharp as he. To present our views and win the case, we had to be thorough in our research and compelling in our arguments. It created, in my view, a culture of excellence in the civil service. Never take short cuts or the intellectually lazy argument, or short-change other points of view. For Mr Lee would sniff out these weaknesses. This culture of analytical rigour, openness to ideas – balanced by realism – infuses the political leadership as much as it does the civil service. It demands high quality thinking and solid work that defines the government to this day.

## THINKING AHEAD

One of the hallmarks of the Singapore government is its emphasis on long-range thinking. Some say that this is possible only because the ruling party has been in power continuously. But this fails to recognise that in fact, long-range thinking does assume that things change. Lee Kuan Yew knows that nothing is static. As a result, economic planning in government has taken on a self-correcting approach. He wrote that "our job was to plan the broad economic objectives and the target periods within which to achieve them. We reviewed these plans regularly and adjusted them as new realities changed the outlook. Infrastructure and the training and education of workers to meet the needs of employers had to be planned years in advance."[9]

This approach is reflected in the government's emphasis on thinking ahead systematically, planning strategically and then adjusting along the way as circumstances change.

## LEARNING FROM OTHERS, LEARNING FROM THE BEST

"The Singapore economy," Mr Lee has written, "was in very poor shape after Separation in August 1965. So we asked (Dr Albert) Winsemius to return and advise us on our economic strategy." He described Dr Winsemius as "wise and canny". He said that he learnt from Dr Winsemius "practical lessons on how European and American companies operated, which showed me that Singapore could plug into the global economic system of trade and investments by using their desire for profits. I set out to create the conditions that would enable us to do this and we succeeded."[10]

Mr Lee clearly learnt a lot from Dr Winsemius. In fact, he is open to ideas and not dogmatic. But he has a critical view of the negative effects of governance in the West. He wrote, "I stressed that freedom could only exist in an orderly state, not when there was continuous contention or anarchy. In Eastern societies the main objective was to have a well-ordered society so that everyone could enjoy his freedom to the maximum. Parts of contemporary American society were totally unacceptable to Asians because they represented a breakdown of civil society with guns, drugs, violent crime, vagrancy and vulgar public behaviour... America should not foist its system indiscriminately on other societies where it would not work."[11]

Despite this view, he acknowledges that "if we did not have the good points of the West to guide us, we wouldn't have got out of our backwardness. We would have been a backward economy with a backward society. But we do not want all of the West."[12]

But it is not all about learning the best practices of others. Mr Lee also said: "If we don't learn from other people's errors, costly errors, we would be ruined, wouldn't we? We have got very little margin to spare."[13] He explained: "I learnt from negative examples. ... There are thousands of other cities and we can see the mistakes they have made. We can also see what they have done right."[14]

The real wisdom is to know what advice to accept, and to know what will not work in the Singaporean context. This approach has been embraced by the government in every sphere – learn from others, learn from the best. Changi Airport was designed by the Public Works Department (PWD), but with ideas and experiences gleaned from the best airports of the day – like Frankfurt and Amsterdam.

I see Mr Lee as a one-man intelligence agency. During my time in the Foreign Ministry, which has oversight of protocol matters, I noticed that he would meet all kinds of people – people with interesting insights and not just those on the protocol list. I surmise that from these meetings he would integrate their views and insights, but form his own conclusions. He once said: "You must not overlook the importance of discussions with knowledgeable people. I would say that is much more productive than absorbing or running through masses of documents. Because in a short exchange, you can abstract from someone who has immense knowledge and experience, the essence of what he had gained."[15] These interactions help him to hone his judgements, acquire new insights and sharpen his arguments.

## POLICY IS IMPLEMENTATION, IMPLEMENTATION IS POLICY

On making his vision of a garden city come true, Lee Kuan Yew became personally involved in the project of transforming Singapore from just concrete and steel to concrete, steel, trees, shrubs, flowers and parks. He became personally knowledgeable about soil and vegetation, trees and drainage, climate and fertilisers. He surveyed the world for ideas, taking advantage of his travels abroad to look out for them.

I recall receiving a message from Mr Lee's office when I was in the Ministry of Defence. He had driven past Khatib Camp, which was then being redeveloped as the Singapore Armed Forces (SAF) artillery complex. He noticed that the open space in the camp was sparsely planted, and what trees existed were mere saplings. The fenceline had no vegetation. He then sent a memo to the ministry asking why we had not planted the trees earlier, so that they would be more mature by the time the new camp was commissioned. He also said that we should have planted at the fenceline, plants that grew quickly and densely, to provide privacy for the camp. In that short note, he provided the botanical names of the trees and plants that he thought would be suitable for Khatib Camp. Apart from this awe-inspiring familiarity with all these botanical details, it struck me then how serious he was about greening Singapore.

*Peter Ho*

95

To its credit, the Ministry of Defence hoisted in the lessons of this small incident. Later projects, including the SAFTI Military Institute and Changi Naval Base, had comprehensive plans to maintain and even expand the greenery. You could say it became part of military doctrine.

Mr Lee is not a micro-manager. But if something matters to him, he is prepared to roll up his sleeves and show the way. This is leadership by example, and leadership from the front. There is a legendary episode, in 1967, in which he gathered ministers and senior civil servants to talk about the importance of clear and simple written English. Today, this might sound very quaint, but this one encounter had the desired impact.

Mr Lee's attention to detail, while keeping the big picture in mind, has taught us in government that when making policies, the effective implementation of policies is as important as their making. The devil is in the detail. That is why in the civil service today, we say, "policy is implementation, and implementation is policy".

## PEOPLE AND LEADERSHIP

Lee Kuan Yew once wrote: "My experience of developments in Asia has led me to conclude that we need good men to have good government. However good the system of government, bad leaders will bring harm to their people. On the other hand, I have seen several societies well-governed in spite of poor systems of government, because good, strong leaders were in charge."[16]

Many years ago, when I was training to be an army officer under the SAF Overseas Scholarship scheme, I was summoned to the Istana together with Teo Chee Hean. We – two young 18-year-old officer cadets – presented ourselves to Prime Minister Lee. He told us that the Maritime Command, as the Navy was then called, needed to be beefed up and he wanted us to go over from the Army.

Needless to say, it was an intimidating encounter for the two of us. When he asked us at the end of the meeting to give it a try, it was hard to say anything at all except to gulp and nod in agreement. We landlubbers went on to join the Maritime Command. Teo Chee Hean became Chief of Navy and I held a more modest position as Head of Naval Plans. But only Mr Lee will be able to say whether his brief encounter with two young officer cadets was worth the trouble.

Nevertheless, when I look back to those days, I see the prime minister making it his business to build up the Navy and to get good people into it. But it was not that Mr Lee was trying to press-gang us into joining the Maritime Command. Instead, by meeting two lowly officer cadets, he demonstrated his brand of leadership. If something is important to him, he does not just take a personal interest but also makes sure that the system is properly resourced by the right people and the right leaders. It is a lesson I took with me throughout my career in the public service. In this regard, Mr Lee would emphasise: "The single decisive factor that made for Singapore's development was the ability of its ministers and the high quality of the civil servants who supported them."[17]

But as prime minister, he demanded a lot of his people in government. Describing his consternation upon discovering that light switches in a government bungalow did not work, he said: "I want to make sure that every button works and even if you are using it only once in a while, please make sure every morning that it works. And if it doesn't when I happen to be around, then somebody is going to be in for a tough time because I do not want sloppiness... I do not ask of you more than I am prepared to give myself. And I say it does you no harm whatsoever just to make sure that the thing works. And don't be too kind. If you want to be kind to your people, to our people, then you have got to be firm. And at times, stern to those who have a duty to perform to see that the duty is performed."

I think the civil service and its people absorbed his almost obsessive focus on quality and excellence. The Public Service Change Movement (PS21) reflects this. It is not so much that perfection can ever be achieved, but one must learn from mistakes and constantly strive to improve. It is a dominant characteristic of the civil service today.

Early on, he laid out the important quality required of leadership, which is "character – whether your melting point is low or high; whether you believe enough and fervently in what you have to do, to go through a great deal of trial and tribulation".[18] He also felt that "a leader without the vision, to strive to improve things, is no good. Then you'll just stay put, you won't progress."[19]

And of course, on incorruptibility and integrity, he stressed: "The moment key leaders are less than incorruptible, less than stern in demanding high standards, from that moment the structure of administrative integrity will weaken, and eventually crumble. Singapore can survive only if ministers and senior officers are incorruptible and efficient."[20]

The recent spate of scandals in the Singapore Public Service should be seen in this context. That these scandals occurred is regrettable and are stains on the reputation of the service. But that these scandals, however embarrassing, were prosecuted with full transparency should reassure observers that there has been no slackening in the emphasis on integrity and incorruptibility.

## CONCLUSION

Lee Kuan Yew's style of governance can be described as both hard-headed and hard-nosed, but ultimately aimed at producing good results for the community and the nation. As he once said: "There may be times when, in the interest of the whole community, we may have to take steps that are unpopular with a section of the community. On such occasions, remember that the principle which guides our actions is that the paramount interest of the whole community must prevail."[21]

As prime minister, Mr Lee shaped the government to reflect his priorities and beliefs. Incorruptibility, doing what is right and not merely popular, pragmatism and providing long-term vision are the foundational beliefs that he instilled in the civil service. The emphasis on developing our people, on strong and effective leadership, and the core values of integrity, service and excellence arguably derive from Mr Lee's influence and impact.

My generation of civil servants, and the generation before – especially the more senior ones who have had direct and indirect contact with Lee Kuan Yew – are profoundly influenced by his views, his values and his vision.

But in the future, new generations of civil servants will run the government who would never have had the privilege of interacting with Lee Kuan Yew. The question then is whether the DNA of the Singapore Public Service, shaped by his influence and impact, will change. I have pondered this question for a long time. Nothing is immutable. But I think Mr Lee's influence on government in Singapore is so deep and profound that the ethos of the Singapore Public Service will demonstrate a remarkable resilience.

## Endnotes

**1** Lee Kuan Yew, press conference, 9 August 1965. *The Papers of Lee Kuan Yew: Speeches, Interviews and Dialogues, vol. 3: 1965–1966* (Singapore: Gale Asia, 2012), pp. 3–15, at pp. 10–11.

**2** Lee Kuan Yew, *The Singapore Story: Memoirs of Lee Kuan Yew* (Singapore: Singapore Press Holdings, 1998), p. 301.

**3** Ibid., p. 501.

**4** Han Fook Kwang, Warren Fernandez, Sumiko Tan, *Lee Kuan Yew: The Man and His Ideas* (Singapore: Times Editions, 1998), p. 16.

5 Ibid., p. 157.

6 Lee Kuan Yew, "The Fundamentals of Singapore's Foreign Policy: Then and Now", speech at the S Rajaratnam Lecture, 9 April 2009. *The Papers of Lee Kuan Yew: Speeches, Interviews and Dialogues, vol. 18: 2008–2009* (Singapore: Gale Asia, 2013), pp. 400–406, at p. 401.

7 Lee Kuan Yew, speech at the First Annual Dinner of the Singapore Advocates and Solicitors Society, 18 March 1967. *The Papers of Lee Kuan Yew: Speeches, Interviews and Dialogues, vol. 4: 1967–1968* (Singapore: Gale Asia, 2012), pp. 34–40, at p. 39.

8 Han Fook Kwang, Warren Fernandez, Sumiko Tan, *Lee Kuan Yew: The Man and His Ideas* (Singapore: Times Editions, 1998), p. 340; *Hansard*, 1 November 1994, col. 820.

9 Lee Kuan Yew, *From Third World to First: The Singapore Story 1965–2000* (Singapore: Singapore Press Holdings, 2000), p. 85.

10 Lee Kuan Yew, tribute to Dr Albert Winsemius: "Singapore is indebted to Winsemius: SM", *The Straits Times*, 10 December 1996.

11 Lee Kuan Yew, interview with Fareed Zakaria, 5 January 1994. *The Papers of Lee Kuan Yew: Speeches, Interviews and Dialogues, vol. 11: 1990–1994* (Singapore: Gale Asia, 2013), pp. 507–518, at p. 507.

12 Ibid., p. 518.

13 *Hansard*, 19 March 1991, col. 821.

14 Lee Kuan Yew , interview with Liu Thai Ker, 31 August 2012. *Urban Solutions*, 2 (Centre for Liveable Cities, February 2013), p. 10.

15 Han Fook Kwang, Warren Fernandez, Sumiko Tan, *Lee Kuan Yew: The Man and His Ideas* (Singapore: Times Editions, 1998), p. 233.

16 Lee Kuan Yew, *From Third World to First: The Singapore Story 1965–2000* (Singapore: Singapore Press Holdings, 2000), p. 735.

17 Ibid., p. 736.

18 Lee Kuan Yew, speech at a meeting at the Consultation on Youth Leadership Training at Queen Street Methodist Church, 10 April 1967. *The Papers of Lee Kuan Yew: Speeches, Interviews and Dialogues, vol. 4: 1967–1968* (Singapore: Gale Asia, 2012), pp. 59–65, at p. 63.

19 Han Fook Kwang, Warren Fernandez, Sumiko Tan, *Lee Kuan Yew: The Man and His Ideas* (Singapore: Times Editions, 1998), p. 231.

20 Lee Kuan Yew, "What of the Past is Relevant to the Future?", *Petir*, 25th Anniversary Special Issue, 1979, pp. 30–43, at p. 39.

21 Lee Kuan Yew, *The Singapore Story: Memoirs of Lee Kuan Yew* (Singapore: Singapore Press Holdings, 1998), p. 309.

# THE MAKING OF THE
# SINGAPORE PUBLIC SERVICE

———

*Yong Ying-I*

LEE KUAN YEW'S role as the architect of Singapore's success is well known. While Peter Ho's essay draws attention to Mr Lee's impact on governance by setting the tone, pace and direction, I want to focus specifically on Mr Lee's role in building the public service and making it a key element of Singapore's success. His impact extends beyond the influence of a strong personality on a group of trusted public servants. More than two decades after Mr Lee stepped down as prime minister and two years after he left the Cabinet, we still see the influence of his values and thinking on the Singapore Public Service. His ideas have had a lasting influence on the way the public service operates today, because they have been institutionalised in our public service processes and framework, and internalised in our values, ethos and culture.

In this essay I would like to discuss Mr Lee's influence on the Singapore Public Service in three areas: who we are; how we think about issues; and what we believe.

## WHO WE ARE: THE SEARCH FOR TALENT

When I meet my counterparts from ex-British colonies, I am struck by how similar our civil service structures are: whether Australia, Malaysia, Hong

Kong or India, the basic set-ups of our public services and the ways in which they function are very similar. Common features include a permanent civil service separate from elected politicians; an independent public service commission that oversees public service appointments; and ministries led by permanent secretaries with similar roles and remits.

Yet we are very different in one key respect. The Singapore Public Service benefited from Mr Lee's strong belief that the public service must be staffed by some of the finest talent in each generation. In a speech to the public service in 1965, Mr Lee said that Singapore could only survive on the basis of quality, not quantity. He explained, for example, why it was important that the calibre of our judges and prosecutors was as high as, if not higher than, the calibre of defence counsels:

> You get an income tax case and your government advocate is mediocre. The other chap, having half a million dollars at stake with the tax man, employs the best lawyer in town who sweats a whole month on the case. He presents it succinctly, decisively and convincingly and you lose half a million dollars in tax collection.[1]

He worried that "if the law of evidence is loaded against the prosecution plus brains of the defendant being loaded against the prosecution, then thieves, rogues and vagabonds get away. That is not my idea of good government."[2]

Mr Lee's determination to recruit the best led the Singapore government to keenly pursue the brightest students in each cohort, a practice that continues today. The Public Service Commission (PSC) offers top students, who also have the passion to serve Singaporeans, scholarships to the world's most famous universities. Scholars are tracked on their joining the civil service and fast-tracked upwards if they perform well. The PSC and public

*Yong Ying-I*

103

sector human resource system also ensure that appointments to top jobs and promotions within the service are by merit and not by connections. Mr Lee argued that:

> If you want Singapore to succeed ... you must have a system that enables the best man and the most suitable to go into the job that needs them ... You must have an open recruitment system, proper appraisal systems, not just go by word of mouth of some individuals.[3]

I hardly need point out that this is easy to say, hard to do and harder still to sustain over time. Not deviating from this system of meritocracy requires each generation of top leaders in politics, in the PSC and in the government to sustain it. Beliefs take time to be internalised. This belief in meritocracy was borne out by how adamantly Mr Lee felt throughout his four decades in office against allowing individual politicians, civil service leaders, or influential people to intervene and appoint their friends and family.

A key factor in attracting and retaining top talent is salaries. This has been a long established principle in human resource management, but is hard to apply in government because citizens are leery of paying public servants top salaries. Yet Mr Lee staunchly championed – and continues to do so till this day – competitive salaries to attract and retain talent in the public service. What is often highlighted publicly are the salaries of political leaders and administrative officers who lead the public service; what is less often highlighted is that we pay competitive salaries for *all* jobs and *all* schemes of service across the entire public service. This has enabled us to professionalise jobs across the whole public service, whether it is teachers, policemen, nurses, statisticians, accountants, lawyers or IT managers. We even give performance-based bonuses, a practice that distinguishes the Singapore government from virtually all other governments. Competitive market salaries have also enabled us to fight and eliminate systemic corruption. Mr Lee said in a speech in 2005 that ministers and government officers

> have enormous powers to grant or deny permits that can make or break businesses... Whether it is policemen, immigration officers, customs officers or officers in charge of dispensing licences, it is dangerous to have them grossly underpaid.

He argued in this speech that paying civil servants salaries close to what their peers earned in the private sector "enabled them to live according to their station in society without extra sources of illicit income".[4]

Mr Lee was concerned not only with the recruitment and retention of talented public servants, but also with the resilience of the public service with regard to leadership renewal. He often observed how the 1947 assassination of Burmese leader Aung San and his Cabinet changed the course of Burmese history. He said it was "our business to ensure that there are effective alternative leaderships; and that in any case, whatever happens, it is never possible to scrub out the whole leadership".[5]

Mr Lee believes in keeping the public service youthful to build resilience. Hence by design our public service leaders and military leaders retire at a relatively young age. Term limits on senior appointments allow for leadership renewal and encourage talented people to join. Mr Lee also believes that younger people are more up to date in professions where knowledge advances rapidly. When he opened the newly renovated Singapore General

Yong Ying-I

105

Hospital (SGH) in 1981, he said the same principle of self-renewal applied to the medical profession. He said: "Let us get younger men and women in their 30s and 40s. Get them to take on the responsibilities of helping to train our young graduates in their 20s."[6] Mr Lee practises what he preaches – he himself chooses to consult younger doctors in their early 40s because they are up to date with new discoveries and methods.

Most crucially, the public service today is technocratically excellent, world-class and professional because it was significantly insulated from politics in Singapore shortly after independence. In her 1975 analysis, "Politics in an Administration State", Ambassador Chan Heng Chee described the systematic depoliticisation and de-emphasis on competitive politics in Singapore.[7] There are advantages and disadvantages of such a system, but the limiting of adversarial politics has given us the space and time to focus on the long-term, to build capabilities that over time have created this technocratic excellence. Becoming a world-class public administration requires patient nurturing and unwavering commitment to investment over decades, whether it is in talent, infrastructure or organisational capacity. Capabilities are easier to build if one is not navigating choppy political waters and changing direction frequently. We were fortunate these conditions existed in Singapore.

## HOW WE THINK: A CULTURE OF EXCELLENCE

Building a culture of excellence goes beyond having talent. It requires public servants with a genuine passion and sense of mission to build a better Singapore. It also requires public servants who care about the nitty-gritty of policy implementation. On inculcating a sense of public spiritedness among public servants and engaging them, Mr Lee said:

106

Especially for political leaders, you've got to have people work for you and work with you. You've got to enthuse them with the same fire and the same eagerness that pushes you along. I think that is a very big factor in leadership... at the end of the day, you must also have the idealism to succeed, to make people come with you. You must have that vision of what is at the bottom of the rainbow you want to reach. But you must have a sense of reality... to feel when this vision is not practical, that it will ruin us.[8]

To ensure that the public service was working towards the same shared objectives, Mr Lee continually engaged the civil service, spoke with them on issues topmost on his mind and explained his thinking. In the early days, he took civil servants on his community visits to engage residents and understand their concerns so that the civil servants too could better understand ground problems. The book published to commemorate the 50th anniversary of the People's Association mentions that staff from the Prime Minister's Office would collect written requests from residents – enough to fill a large bag.[9] These would be sent to the appropriate departments for action. There are also many notes of meetings from the 1970s onwards where he gathered Members of Parliament, permanent secretaries and senior and younger administrative officers to discuss how Singapore was to progress over the longer term. It was not one-way communication – people were invited to speak from the floor and contribute their ideas.

Mr Lee also built a culture of excellence by demanding that public servants give attention to detail. The public service has been taught that "policy is implementation and implementation is policy". The real test of an excellent concept or vision is its translation into reality. To the generations of public service leaders who worked with Mr Lee, his interest in and grasp of details are legendary and his high performance standards bracing.

When I served as permanent secretary in the Ministry of Manpower, for example, I was struck by how much effort and care Mr Lee had put into designing the industrial relations framework in Singapore, to give us the best chance of being a harmonious society. Mr Lee's work with the unions has been documented.[10] He also designed systems and processes within government to promote harmonious industrial relations. For example, he designed the Labour Court to drive towards settlement of disputes between employers and employees. No lawyers are to be present in the court, because this would encourage an adversarial approach; no fees are required for court hearings so that parties do not face obstacles to settling disputes; in the meantime, so long as the route to settlement exists, workers must try to take it and not go on strike.

I vividly recall our considering introducing escalating court charges for long-drawn-out cases – to promote efficiency and avoid wasting the courts' time – and being told by Mr Lee that we should read the history of the design before tinkering with it! Mr Lee said that the most important priority was "to give companies and workers no excuse not to settle". The institutionalisation of systems and processes requires subsequent generations of civil servants to understand the roots of our approaches and what has made us successful, so that we do not inadvertently dismantle them.

Mr Lee also paid attention to issues that can be overlooked but that have great impact, for example, clear communication. During a meeting in February 1979, he gathered permanent secretaries and "everybody who has to do with the drafting of minutes, memoranda, Cabinet papers and other documents that go up to ministers" to discuss the "importance of simple, clear, written English".[11] Mr Lee said at the meeting:

> When you write notes, minutes or memos, do not write in code, so that only those privy to your thoughts can understand. Write so simply that any other officer who knows nothing of the subject can still understand you.[12]

When he visits various parts of Singapore, he is known to call up senior public servants to ask about matters as varied as why this tree is doing poorly and why that area is so dirty and poorly maintained. He would send memos. As an example of his penchant for details, he wrote in 1969:

> Zoo Negara says that it costs $210 a month to feed a rhino, $200 a tiger or a lion, and $160 a polar bear. I do not believe sick dogs being shot can form a substitute for a regular meat supply, which will have to be paid for. There are very few zoos in the world which are successful and I am doubtful of the wisdom of starting one in Singapore.[13]

On another occasion in the 1960s, Mr Lee wrote to the permanent secretary for National Development:

> We spoke the other day about the maintenance of jets, nozzles and pressure of all our public fountains. Make sure something is done to see that pressures are maintained and nozzles kept clean, every six months or year as the case may be, and the pattern never altered.[14]

Wong Woon Liong, former director-general of the Civil Aviation Authority of Singapore, remembers that Mr Lee wanted from the management a weekly report of the state of cleanliness of the toilets in Paya Lebar Airport. Since the boss wanted a weekly report, Wong decided he had better ask for a daily report. And since he wanted a daily report, the director for operations asked for an hourly report. So that is why we have clean toilets in airports – a tradition that continues today at Changi Airport.

I myself had quite a few personal encounters with Mr Lee in my previous posting as permanent secretary for health. I can confirm his attention to detail and concern for high standards. He gave me feedback about the choice and quality of trees planted on the SGH campus in Outram and at Tan Tock Seng Hospital in Novena. When I accompanied Mr Lee to visit the new Khoo Teck Puat Hospital a few years ago, he asked the hospital chief executive numerous questions about health-care delivery and serving patients. He then asked me about the problems with the building design. For example, he wanted to know whether the corridors got wet when it rained – they did – and whether the building might be less warm if we improved the planting of creepers down some of the walls. He even wanted to know whether the pond next to the hospital flooded and overflowed to the hospital when it rained. The answer, fortunately, was no. This attention to detail by the boss matters. If the boss cares, everybody else up and down the line cares. If the boss does not care, standards can begin to slip.

Besides a culture of excellence undergirded by public spiritedness and an emphasis on implementation, Mr Lee also believed in pragmatism, not ideology. This includes how he saw the partnership between the public service and the political leadership in serving Singapore. In 1959, he spoke to civil service leaders to make clear his expectations of how politicians and civil servants were to work together in serving Singapore:

My theme to you is simply this. You and I have a vested interest in the survival of the democratic state. We the elected ministers have to work through you and with you to translate our plans and policies into reality. You should give of your best in the service of our people. Whatever your views on socialism, capitalism, liberalism, communism, whether they be progressive or conservative, your task and mine for the next five years are exactly the same: that is, to demonstrate that the democratic system can produce results. It is in our interest to show that under the system of "one man, one vote" there can be an honest and efficient government which works through an efficient administration in the interests of our people.

If we do not do our best, then we only have ourselves to blame when the people lose faith, not just in you, the public service, and in us, the democratic political leadership, but also in the democratic system of which you and I are working parts...

I am confident that... you will respond to the urgency of the task. The mass of the people are not concerned with legal and constitutional forms and niceties. They are not interested in the theory of the separation of powers and the purpose and function of a politically neutral public service under such a constitution. As far as they are concerned, in May 1959... they did elect their own government in order that there might be a better world for them and their children.[15]

## WHAT WE BELIEVE: INTERNALISING MR LEE'S VALUES
Mr Lee's influence in shaping the values and ethos of the public service has been enormous. Many of his personal values have become our institutional values, heavily shaping how we are run internally today. Mr Lee believes

in "getting the economics right". This includes living within one's means; getting value for money from our purchases; keeping subsidies limited; not protecting weak performers; frowning on cross-subsidies which fudge true costs.

Mr Lee is a model for these beliefs and tenets of value for money, thrift and frugality: his office and home are furnished simply; he does not have a huge wardrobe of clothes and neither does his immediate family; he entertains foreign dignitaries comfortably, but not lavishly. The government does not have its own plane, yachts, houses and other frills of office for ministers and officials. Ministers and civil servants fly on normal commercial airlines. Singapore Airlines (SIA) has been instructed never to hold a plane for any minister who is late; he will just have to miss the flight. SIA also does not give upgrades to civil servants.

112    The public service takes its cue accordingly so that value for money, thrift and frugality are the tenets for how the public service is run. We have tight controls on the size of offices and office decorations, on receiving gifts or giving them, and on discretionary expenditures such as entertainment and travel. A new manager who thinks that we are now a First World country and ought to spend accordingly will find himself reined in and quietly reminded that "this is not done here".

It is worth noting that there is a distinction between systemic corruption and ad hoc corruption by individuals. We do not have systemic corruption. The 2012 edition of Transparency International's Corruption Perceptions Index, for example, ranks Singapore fifth for having a clean government.[16] The key policy supporting the prevention of systemic corruption is our "clean wage" policy. Mr Lee guided the service away from providing staff quarters and staff cars very early on and we began moving away from pensions as early as 1973. Today, there are virtually no hidden benefits or "overheads".

Learning from Mr Lee, the public service has not just avoided systemic corruption, but also taken on the role of an honest steward. The paper by Ambassador Chan cited earlier discussed the power of the bureaucracy in an administrative state. It observed that we had built over the decades a powerful military-industrial-administration complex, where powerful bureaucrats exerted significant influence over the whole structure. Those days are long gone, with the privatisation and listing of many businesses and the reduced involvement of serving civil servants in most of these businesses. The more important point is that, unlike virtually every other country, the bureaucracy succeeded in delivering successful professionally run companies – Singapore Technologies, Keppel, SIA and so many more – and then we succeeded in devolving power, in drawing in professionals and deliberately withdrawing from control. The ethos is "honest stewardship". To use power for the right purpose and to be able to give it up and withdraw at the right time is a critically important ethos we have learnt from Mr Lee.

Related to this is Mr Lee's aversion to personality cults. There are no streets or buildings named after him. We only have two schools of learning named after him – the Lee Kuan Yew School of Public Policy at the National University of Singapore and the Lee Kuan Yew Centre for Innovative Cities at the Singapore University of Technology and Design. Kishore Mahbubani, dean of the LKY School of Public Policy, said that when the school was set up, Mr Lee emphasised to him that it should be the LKY School of Public Policy and not the LKY School of Thought. Mr Lee is totally against self-aggrandisement and that ethos pervades the political leadership and public service.

Yet Mr Lee's magnetic personality and leadership drew outstanding

*Yong Ying-I*

113

people to work with him – men like JY Pillay, George Bogaars, Sim Kee Boon, Lim Siong Guan and many more who have not only been technically able, but also entrepreneurial, innovative and realistic. Many of these outstanding people have been quoted as saying that Mr Lee has a zeal that could convert others. Mr Lee is a conviction politician, a superb persuader and mobiliser who persuaded the civil service to believe that what he was fighting for was their fight as well.

Most people tend to think of Mr Lee's philosophy of "getting the economics right" as a hard-nosed, tough-love approach. But a more thoughtful study would show that Mr Lee has always struck a fine balance. There has been emphasis from the earliest days about everyone sharing the fruits of success. Even as he champions meritocracy, Mr Lee speaks about fairness and compassion. In 1972, he spoke on "The Socialist Philosophies Behind Singapore's Development":

114

> We have mitigated the exploitation of man by his fellow men through the possession of wealth. We have not tried to prevent a man doing better than his fellow men through his own ability, training and hard work. Compassion for the less fortunate moves our policies... We can be soft-hearted. But we cannot afford to be soft-headed.[17]

People who have worked closely with him and around him know of his kindness, consideration and interest in people. My family and I have been privileged to have a close friendship with him and his family, and I have always been struck by his kindness and concern, as well as Mrs Lee's care and consideration for everyone around her. Leaders who are merely tough and hard-nosed may achieve success, but they do not inspire the devotion that shines through the essays in this volume.

## AS WE GO FORWARD

To conclude, many of the things we see as fundamental to the public service today have been shaped by Lee Kuan Yew's ideas. And many of these – our technocratic excellence, our emphasis on succession and renewal, our pragmatic approach to policy-making, our ethos of frugality and value for money, our integrity and sense of stewardship – remain sources of strength. As the environment around us evolves, the public service needs to adapt to remain relevant and effective. In this context, going back to read Mr Lee's speeches and advice usually offers breathtaking clarity of purpose that helps us appreciate more deeply what we stand for and where we need to go. In reflecting on what needs to change, the public service leadership has gained the insight that the fundamental principles of governance Mr Lee set out may need to be adapted in their translation and application to the present context, but that they remain fundamental and vital to our future.

*Yong Ying-I*

115

116

## Endnotes

1 Lee Kuan Yew, "Surviving on the Basis of Quality", speech to senior civil servants at Victoria Memorial Hall (30 September 1965), *The Papers of Lee Kuan Yew: Speeches, Interviews and Dialogues, vol. 3: 1965–1966* (Singapore: Gale Asia, 2012), p. 111.

2 Ibid., p. 124.

3 Warren Fernandez, *Without Fear or Favour: 50 Years of Singapore's Public Service Commission* (Singapore: Times Media, 2001), pp. 136–137.

4 Lee Kuan Yew, "Ethical Leadership a Competitive Edge", speech at the World Ethics and Integrity Forum 2005, Kuala Lumpur, 28 April 2005, http://app.cpib.gov.sg/data/website/doc/ManagePage/247/Speech%20of%20Minister%20Mentor.pdf, accessed 1 September 2013.

5 Lee Kuan Yew, "Surviving on the Basis of Quality", speech to senior civil servants at Victoria Memorial Hall (30 September 1965), *The Papers of Lee Kuan Yew: Speeches, Interviews and Dialogues, vol. 3: 1965-1966* (Singapore: Gale Asia, 2012), p. 118.

6 Lee Kuan Yew, "New Mindsets for a New Hospital Building", speech at the opening of the new Singapore General Hospital (SGH) (12 September 1981), *The Papers of Lee Kuan Yew: Speeches, Interviews and Dialogues, vol. 9: 1981-1987* (Singapore: Gale Asia, 2012), p. 70.

7 Chan Heng Chee, "Politics in an Administration State: Where has the Politics Gone?" Paper presented in Singapore at the seminar on Trends in Singapore (1974) (Singapore: University of Singapore, 1975).

8 Han Fook Kwang, Warren Fernandez, Sumiko Tan, *Lee Kuan Yew: The Man and His Ideas* (Singapore: Times Editions, 1998), p. 231.

9 Jimmy Yap, *We are One: The People's Association Journey* (Singapore: Straits Times Press, 2010), p. 77.

10 Lee Kuan Yew, *From Third World to First: The Singapore Story 1965–2000* (Singapore: Singapore Press Holdings, 2000), pp. 103–115. Other accounts include SR Nathan, *Winning Against the Odds: The Labour Research Unit in NTUC's Founding* (Singapore: Straits Times Press, 2011); Raj Vasil, "Trade Unions", in Kernial Singh Sandhu and Paul Wheatley, eds., *Management of Success: The Moulding of Modern Singapore* (Singapore: Institute of Southeast Asian Studies, 1989); and Ee Boon Lee and Leong Ching, *U & Me: Fifty Years of the Labour Movement in Singapore* (Singapore: National Trades Union Congress, 2011).

11 Lee Kuan Yew, "The Importance of Simple, Clear Written English", address to the ministers, ministers of state and senior civil service officers at the Regional Language Centre (RELC) (27 February 1979). *The Papers of Lee Kuan Yew: Speeches, Interviews and Dialogues, vol. 8: 1978-1980* (Singapore: Gale Asia, 2012), p. 285.

12 Ibid., p. 286.

13 Files in the PMO Archive.

14 Files in the PMO Archive.

15 Lee Kuan Yew's speech at the Civil Service Political Study Centre on 15 August 1959, in Han Fook Kwang, Warren Fernandez, Sumiko Tan, *Lee Kuan Yew: The Man and His Ideas* (Singapore: Times Editions, 1998), pp. 318–319.

16 Transparency International, *Corruption Perceptions Index 2012*, http://cpi.transparency.org/cpi2012/, accessed 20 November 2013.

17 Lee Kuan Yew, "The Socialist Philosophies Behind Singapore's Development", address at the opening of the conference of the Asia-Pacific Socialist Bureau of Socialist International at the Singapore Conference Hall (28 May 1972). *The Papers of Lee Kuan Yew: Speeches, Interviews and Dialogues, vol. 6: 1972-1974* (Singapore: Gale Asia, 2012), p. 55.

PART
4

# SOCIETY
# AND
# ECONOMICS

## Bilingualism: A Never-ending Journey

*Seng Han Thong*

## LKY: Notes Towards Defining His Soul-craft

*Janadas Devan*

# BILINGUALISM:
# A NEVER-ENDING JOURNEY

————

*Seng Han Thong*

LEE KUAN YEW has been thinking about language for over 60 years. He has been asking himself three big questions on this topic:

- Should a multiracial and multilingual society like Singapore be bilingual or monolingual?
- Can a person actually master two languages equally well?
- And finally, how far can bilingualism be achieved in reality? In particular, should the push for bilingualism be tempered by practical considerations?

I want to use this essay as an opportunity to examine Mr Lee's thinking on these issues.

## WHY BE BILINGUAL?

What made Mr Lee a strong believer in the idea that Singaporeans must master English and yet also know their mother tongue? In other words, why did Mr Lee push for bilingualism?

I would argue that thoughts along this line were already forming in Mr Lee's mind from a very early stage. Let me take you back to 1947 when he was studying in Cambridge. He would occasionally visit the China Institute in London, a gathering place for students of Chinese ethnicity. As Mr Lee was to later observe:

> I often went there and would see Chinese students from all corners of the world. From their accents, you could tell where they were from – China, Hong Kong, Malaya or Mauritius, for example. The most pitiful were those from the West Indies. They spoke in singsong West Indian "English" and absolutely no Chinese. I felt very sad for them. I vowed that I would not be like them. That was when I began to feel a sense of loss about not knowing Chinese, and decided not to repeat this state of affairs with my own children. What I saw there stayed with me for the rest of my life and fuelled my determination to learn Chinese and push bilingual education in Singapore.[1]

This was not simply about language – it was also part of Mr Lee's political awakening. He began to realise while studying in England that he was not one of them even though he spoke their language. Culturally, he was different. I would argue that it was at this point that he began his search for values too. Much later, Mr Lee said:

> Following my experiences as a student in London and Cambridge, I believe firmly that knowing one's mother tongue is a must. It gives one the sense of belonging to a culture and increases self-confidence and self-respect. Hence, we decided that we must teach each student two languages – English and mother tongue.[2]

Indeed, throughout the decades, Mr Lee has been consistent in his view that a mother tongue provides a foundation for a whole system of values. In 1966, at the opening of a seminar on education and nation-building, he talked

*Seng Han Thong*

about "Language Problems in Schools", and said:

> There is the necessity for preserving for each child that cultural ballast
> and appreciation of his origin and his background in order to give him
> that confidence to face the problems of his society. He must know from
> whence he came and how it is that he is where he is, before he is able
> to meet the problems and make the decisions which he must make to
> adjust himself and his family in the society in which he has decided to
> make a home.[3]

Speaking elsewhere of this value system, Mr Lee has also observed that
the mother tongue gives one a philosophy of life, one that can maintain the
fabric of our society intact, in spite of exposure to passing fads and fashions.

122

### BILINGUALISM IN PRACTICE

What was the backdrop to language education in Singapore when Mr Lee
returned from his studies?

In 1952, the study of vernacular languages was introduced in government
primary schools but was only made compulsory from 1955. Then came the
All-Party Report in 1956 which laid the seeds of bilingual education in
Singapore. The All-Party Report recommended that the future education
system in Singapore should produce students equally conversant in two or
even three of the main languages. The committee was chaired by the minister
for education, Chew Swee Kee, and included legislative assemblymen like
Lim Yew Hock and Lee Kuan Yew. So even from an early stage, Mr Lee was
involved in these debates. And I note in passing that language issues were on
the PAP's agenda from the very start. The PAP founding manifesto in 1954
emphasised the importance of all four languages – English, Malay, Chinese

and Tamil. In 1954, I should add, the PAP was still in the Opposition.

Now, let us move to the key question: how did Mr Lee fare in trying to translate his ideas on bilingualism into reality? While in the Opposition, Mr Lee would have seen the practical difficulties in implementing the All-Party Report. Sensitivities concerning language and ethnicity could literally start a riot. As he was to say later:

> The outbreak of violence among Chinese-medium school students in the 1950s was a constant reminder of what chaos and disruption the students led by leftists and chauvinists could mount when they interpreted the bilingual policy as reducing the primary role of Chinese. We could not make English the first language in all schools at that time – it would have caused a riot. We moved carefully, step by step, to enable parents to realise how English would lift their children's future prospects. Enlightened self-interest would get people to accept our bilingual policy.[4]

This is an important point. Chinese schools taught their curriculum mainly in the Chinese language. Asking the Chinese schools and Chinese educationists to give up Chinese as a teaching medium was a very emotive issue, and politically risky. How did he achieve this? The answer is: slowly, and carefully.

The first step, of course, was the emphasis on English. Mr Lee, from an early stage, was convinced that part of the issue was that Singapore's ethnic groups had to have a common platform to communicate with one another. This is what he had to say on the subject in 1966 when speaking about the various ethnic groups in Singapore:

*Seng Han Thong*

123

You must try to give them common denominators or you will have a situation in which there will be no communication between sectors of your own society. And one decision we made, again I believe rightly, is that in this situation, a person who is [monolingual], competent only in one language, is a problem to himself and to his society. If you know only one language, whatever it may be, Chinese, Malay, Tamil or English, and no other language, then in this society you will find yourself a problem for yourself and for your society. And invariably, you will find that with knowledge of another language, which means an understanding of a different culture, a different civilisation and more windows in the mind, come inevitably, tolerance and understanding. The chauvinist, the bigot, the extremist very often is a monolinguist; his mind has no windows into other worlds.[5]

124

Not many people know Mr Lee was minister for education for four months in 1975. And it was during those four months when Mr Lee was our sixth education minister that he was able to closely scrutinise the education system. He realised that years of promoting bilingualism in schools were not having the desired effect. The majority of students were failing in their language. Only 19 per cent of Primary One students made it through Secondary Four with passes in both first and second language.

I believe that Mr Lee's experience as education minister left an impression on him. By the mid to late 1970s, he had become clear that the one-size-fits-all approach did not work. People have different aptitudes and different home environments. For example, a large part of the 75 per cent ethnic Chinese population had to grapple with three languages – dialects at home, Mandarin and English in school. To solve the problem, the prime minister proposed that Mandarin replace the other Chinese dialects as the language spoken at home. This would also facilitate the learning of Mandarin in schools. The 1979 Goh Keng Swee Report on Education addressed this issue head-on. It stated that "the basic objective of our education system should be to produce school leavers who are literate in at least one language".

The Goh Keng Swee Report introduced streaming for pupils at Primary Three into one of three streams: standard bilingual stream where pupils would do two languages and complete their primary education in six years; extended bilingual stream where pupils would work at a slower pace and complete primary school in eight years; monolingual stream for pupils best suited to vocational or technical careers. This eight-year stream was meant for pupils from English-, Malay- or Tamil-speaking home environments to be taught mainly in English and those from Chinese home environments to do Chinese as their main language with some oral English.

The report was very controversial. The most common complaint was that pupils were streamed too early. Most parents also wanted their children to go into the mainstream six-year programme, not eight years.

The streaming system was reviewed 11 years later in 1990. The committee chaired by John Yip, then director of education, recommended that streaming be done at Primary Four instead of Primary Three and all pupils would go to secondary school. After streaming at Primary Four, there would be three streams from Primary Five to Six:

EM1: English and mother tongue at first language level
EM2: English as first language, mother tongue as second language
EM3: Foundational English, basic proficiency in mother tongue

125

Seng Han Thong

Again, it was noted that Singaporeans whose children were streamed to EM3 were not happy.

One year after the overhaul of the streaming system, then Deputy Prime Minister Ong Teng Cheong headed a committee to look into all aspects of Chinese language learning, from teaching methods and textbooks to curricula and examinations. The committee was formed in June 1991 and its report was published in 1992.

The Ong Teng Cheong Report recommended, among other things, that the Ministry of Education should:

1   Change the name CL2 to Chinese language and CL1 to Higher Chinese to correct the impression that Chinese was not an important subject.

2   Revise Chinese language instructional materials to reflect current trends in language learning and to enhance the learning and appreciation of Chinese culture and traditional values.

3   Teach hanyu pinyin or romanised Chinese earlier, instead of waiting until Primary Four, and allow approved Chinese dictionaries to be used for essay-writing examinations.

Five years later, in 1997, another Chinese Language Review Committee was formed. This time it was headed by Deputy Prime Minister Lee Hsien Loong. The committee recommended three key changes:

1   The introduction of the alternative Chinese Language B syllabus at the upper secondary and junior college levels.

2   The return of Chinese language textbooks to the pre-1991 standard.

3   More students will have a chance to take Higher Chinese Language at first language level.

There were strong reactions to the recommendations. Some felt that these amounted to a rollback of the standard set by the Ong Teng Cheong committee.

Lee Kuan Yew followed the debate that ensued in the wake of Lee Hsien Loong's committee report. Later, he said:

> To me, the crux of the issue was not how easy or difficult the Chinese language syllabus was, but how it was taught. I wanted the Education Ministry to be more open to the idea of using English in the teaching of Chinese.[6]

Mr Lee's attitude is to never give up. His strong will to ensure that a certain basic level of Mandarin is maintained among Singaporeans has never flagged. Also, language is the core of how he defines the Singapore nation-building project. English is the language of the workplace or administration, but our mother tongues help us retain our core cultural values as Chinese, Malay or Indian.

## THE CHALLENGE OF APTITUDE

This discussion on the challenges of implementing bilingual education brings us to a second question: can a person master two languages equally well? This is a sensitive and sometimes emotional issue. Mr Lee eventually concluded that a person may be bilingual or even trilingual, but one language will be the dominant language. This is what he said in 2009:

> At first, I thought you can master two languages... Why did I think that? General principles of intelligence and learning... [But the reality is that] nobody can master two languages at the same level. If you

think you can, you are deceiving yourself. The brain is not structured to have the language capability.[7]

Many will recall the National Day Rallies held when Mr Lee was the prime minister. He had been delivering his National Day Rally speech since 1966, one year after Singapore's independence. He used to deliver his speech in Malay, Hokkien, Mandarin and English. Then the Education Ministry pointed out to him that he was not setting a good example by using Hokkien when schools were trying to teach Mandarin. So his last speech in Hokkien was in 1979. In the same year, on 7 September 1979, three weeks after his last Hokkien speech at the rally, he launched the Speak Mandarin Campaign. At the launch, Mr Lee urged young people – students and graduates – to give up dialects in five years and to have Mandarin, English and Malay become the language of the coffee shops, hawker centres, shops, cinemas and other public places.

Years later, in 2005, when asked if he worried about the political cost of giving up Hokkien as many people were then still speaking dialects, Mr Lee said:

> I had a responsibility not to mislead the young. As long as I was still speaking Hokkien at the National Day Rally, I was in fact saying it is okay to do so. If so, people would never give up Hokkien; they would never move to Mandarin. So the Speak Mandarin Campaign will fail and the learning of Mandarin in schools would never be successful. So never mind the price; setting a good example, it had to be done. Everyone has a limit; you have to decide what do you want to do within your limited capacity and how do you maximise it for your life?[8]

Mr Lee was a tactful leader. This helped him turn English into our main medium of education by the 1980s. However, he was very direct and forthright about the elimination of Hokkien, even at the risk of offending people. As is well known, Mr Lee is very determined when he feels that something is the right thing to do for Singapore. In the case of the use of dialect, ministers such as Lim Kim San and Toh Chin Chye, who were comfortable in dialect, understood the intellectual argument that people had a finite ability to absorb languages. But emotionally, they were not convinced. Lim Kim San pointed out that there was an emotional vacuum as children would not be able to communicate with their dialect-speaking grandparents. Mr Lee realised that there would be a cost, but to leave matters as they were was not tenable; and if there was an emotional loss, then this was a price that had to be paid.

It is important that Mr Lee's emphasis on bilingualism be seen in the context not only of Mandarin-language promotion, but of all the national languages. In general, policies and the various reviews affecting the Chinese language were applied to the other mother tongues as well. As Mr Lee put it:

> It is not just the Chinese language that we must get our people to learn. Malays must learn the Malay language, Tamils their Tamil language. Our schools must teach the basic values and culture of each group's heritage using their mother tongues.[9]

Mr Lee was aware of the sensitivities when the bilingual policy was introduced in 1978. He was aware that minority races might think that this was a ploy to foist Mandarin on them. He sought to calm these fears. Addressing this point in 1979, he acknowledged that these initial fears would be unavoidable. He said then:

> The Malay or the Indian or the Eurasian will say, look, what are we doing? We say we are bilingual but does bilingualism mean English-Mandarin and not English-Malay or English-Tamil? But if, in fact, it is not then it is only a matter of time – whether it will be three months, six months, one year – before the truth dawns on everybody that no, no non-Chinese needs to learn Mandarin or needs to be at a disadvantage.[10]

Understanding these sensitivities, and being bilingual, was also good politics. Part of the PAP's success can be attributed to the fact that it has always been the party for all races and all the official languages – as evidenced by the party's founding constitution mentioned earlier – and the party has remained true to this commitment.

In March 1992, then Senior Minister Lee launched the Mandarin-speaking luncheon for ministers at the Istana. Senior journalists from the Chinese press, including myself, were invited to join in the lunch. Present at the inauguration lunch were PM Goh Chok Tong, Minister for Education Lee Yock Suan, Minister for Information and the Arts George Yeo, Minister for Labour Dr Lee Boon Yang and Minister for Communications Mah Bow Tan. I recall that a week before the launch, Goh Chok Tong shared with us that the conversation during these luncheon meetings would be entirely in Mandarin. The idea was to force him and other ministers to discuss current affairs in Mandarin with people from Chinese-speaking backgrounds. This would help them overcome the psychological barrier, pick up more Chinese vocabulary, especially on politics and economics, and form a habit of speaking Mandarin more naturally without inhibitions. Once they gained enough confidence, they would start doing this in public. Of course, all this would be done without causing uneasiness among the minorities.

Did their Mandarin improve? I would say that Goh Chok Tong really put in the effort to learn Mandarin and his Mandarin improved over the years as could be seen from his annual National Day Rally Mandarin speeches.

You may also ask: are all ministers effectively bilingual? The answer is No. This shows the difficulties of language learning, but the fact is that they persisted, and it was important that they could communicate with citizens in their mother tongue.

## CONCLUSION

Let me attempt to summarise some core principles that guide Mr Lee's thinking after half a century of trial and error with our bilingual policy.

**Principle One:** Language policy is a vital instrument for achieving national interest objectives and meeting the needs of governance.

**Principle Two:** Language policy can make or break a nation. By choosing English as our language of administration, we managed to avoid the political fallout had we chosen Malay over Chinese or Chinese over Malay.

**Principle Three:** Language is more than a tool of communication; it transmits values too. That is why we have insisted that all school-going children learn their mother tongue – Chinese, Malay or Tamil – as their second language.

Language is at the core of how Lee Kuan Yew defines the Singapore nation-building project. English is the language of the workplace or administration, but our mother tongue helps us retain our core cultural values as Chinese, Malay or Indian.

At the same time, it is a never-ending journey. Our bilingual policy continues to evolve. Indeed language policy must evolve as society progresses, in order to remain relevant and to ensure that it remains true to the first principle – that language policy is a vital instrument for achieving national interest objectives and meeting the needs of governance.

Many Singaporeans of the present generation have gone through this journey at different points in time. In the process, we have built up a large and complex language laboratory providing various models and examples for other multilingual countries' reference and for sociologists and language-planning studies.

After 50 years of observing the world while striving to build Singapore into a First World nation, Mr Lee has come to the conclusion that our decision to have a bilingual education system was the right one. He noted that we did not get it right from the start. We went through many years of trial and error and learnt hard lessons along the way, but this did not mean our work is done. Education policy, especially pertaining to language, will always be a work in progress. As Mr Lee put it:

> No policy in Singapore has undergone so many adjustments and reviews as our policy on the teaching of mother tongue and in particular the Chinese language. These have been necessary to maintain that dynamic balance between the needs of the country and the concerns and preferences of individuals and communities.[11]

## Endnotes

1 Lee Kuan Yew, *My Lifelong Challenge, Singapore's Bilingual Journey* (Singapore: Straits Times Press, 2011), p. 32.

2 Lee Kuan Yew, *My Lifelong Challenge*, p. 60.

3 *The Papers of Lee Kuan Yew: Speeches, Interviews and Dialogues, vol. 3: 1965–1966* (Singapore: Gale Asia, 2012), p. 605.

4 Lee Kuan Yew, *My Lifelong Challenge*, p. 60.

5 "Language Problems in Schools", speech at the opening of seminar on education and nation-building, 27 December 1966. *The Papers of Lee Kuan Yew: Speeches, Interviews and Dialogues, vol. 3: 1965–1966* (Singapore: Gale Asia, 2012), p. 604.

6 Lee Kuan Yew, *My Lifelong Challenge*, p. 189.

7 Speech at the opening of the Singapore Centre for Chinese Language, 17 November 2009. *The Papers of Lee Kuan Yew: Speeches, Interviews and Dialogues, vol. 19: 2009–2011* (Singapore: Gale Asia, 2013), p. 151.

8 Chua Chee Lay, ed., *Keeping My Mandarin Alive: Lee Kuan Yew's Language Learning Experience* (Singapore: World Scientific, 2005), p. 37.

9 Lee Kuan Yew, *My Lifelong Challenge*, p. 71.

10 "Language Competence and Multilingual Societies – A Discussion with the Prime Minister", 20 November 1979. *The Papers of Lee Kuan Yew: Speeches, Interviews and Dialogues, vol. 8: 1978–1980* (Singapore: Gale Asia, 2012), p. 411.

11 Lee Kuan Yew, *My Lifelong Challenge*, p. 170.

# LKY: NOTES TOWARDS DEFINING HIS SOUL-CRAFT

---

*Janadas Devan*

WHAT EXPLAINS SINGAPORE'S startling progress from Third World to First? Can the "Singapore model" be reduced to a few general principles? Can it be replicated elsewhere, like a piece of machinery – and without the informing genius of the country's chief architects and statesmen, most particularly Lee Kuan Yew?

Many, even well-informed and sympathetic observers of Singapore, think it can. Consider, for instance, Henri Ghesquiere's well-regarded *Singapore's Success: Engineering Economic Growth*. "Engineering prosperity is at the heart of Singapore," he writes. "Engineering is central to Singapore."[1]

The idea that Singapore owes its success to engineering – the fitting together, as in a machine, of various pieces of economic, social and political policies; the idea that Singapore *is* that engineered artefact – is what, in Dr Ghesquiere's view, explains the country's success:

> The political elite's passionate pursuit of shared prosperity required assembling together many diverse components ... to create an intricate and highly effective mechanism ... [The] work ethic and delayed gratification of postponing consumption, exposure to market

competition, meritocracy in schooling and civil service, public integrity, and law and order have all served as essential lubricants.[2]

Singapore's political leaders, in this version of history, began with an "overarching emphasis on achieving sustained prosperity".[3] Then, like engineers, they looked around for components and parts, levers and hinges to produce that prosperity. Thus nation-building was for them a function of prosperity. Political and social stability, ethnic and religious harmony, equal opportunity and social justice – none of these was an end in itself, but a means to "engineer" wealth.

Could that have been possible? Were Mr Lee and his Old Guard colleagues primarily engineers and only secondarily statesmen? Could they in 1959, when Mr Lee became prime minister at the age of 35, have conceived of the Singapore of 55 years later, down to its last particular? Could they really have set forth with a blueprint for prosperity, filled with precise specifications?

Racial harmony and social justice to buttress the base of the machine; political and social stability to encase it; a bolt of family values, a component of work ethic and a screw of industrial harmony; a CPF lever over here, an EDB hinge over there, an SAF undergirding and plenty of HDB lubricant – and *abracadabra!* we've got a machine for producing happiness.

It is admittedly difficult to escape the machine metaphor in discussing Singapore. Just as the inevitable analogue of a well-run office is a neatly organised filing cabinet, the equivalent of a smoothly functioning economic system would seem to be the internal combustion engine. Insofar as planning and foresight, and attention to detail and structure defines the Singapore model, a social scientist describing the country would find it

*Janadas Devan*

135

all but impossible not to fall back on the engineering metaphor. Still, the metaphor is misleading, if not wholly inaccurate. It most certainly misstates the role of Singapore's founding fathers.

Firstly, there was no blueprint. It is simply impossible that Mr Lee and his colleagues could have foreseen every particular of the system they created. Interestingly, the Old Guard had among them lawyers and economists, journalists and trade unionists, scientists and entrepreneurs, but no engineers. They did not achieve what they did by working off a blueprint. There was a good deal of trial and error. The fact that they did not commit a large number of crippling errors does not mean there wasn't plenty of trial.

Secondly, the engineering metaphor implies a manual – but none existed. No manual-toting group of politicians would have thought of combining MNCs with GLCs, or of splicing a "socialism that works" (Dr Goh Keng Swee's formulation) with a capitalist free-market economy, which is now judged by the World Economic Forum to be more competitive than Japan's or Britain's. If Mr Lee and his colleagues were engineers, they were innovators, not mechanics.

And finally, the engineering metaphor – the notion that "engineering is central to Singapore" – ignores the confusing boom and buzz of history. Singapore did not get to 2014 in a straight-line trajectory from 1959. There were diversions and detours, cul-de-sacs and dangerous passages.

Two in particular must be stressed, for they shaped Mr Lee (and Singapore) in fundamental ways. If one were to specify the non-economic factors behind Singapore's economic growth, one would find their source in these two historical tragedies.

The first was the People's Action Party's near-death experience in 1961, when it was almost defeated by the radical left. In retrospect, it was fortunate that the PAP had such formidable opponents. Precisely because the communists had such dedicated, courageous and honest cadres, Mr Lee had to insist on high standards of probity within his own ranks. Precisely because the communists had such an astoundingly strong hold of the ground, the PAP had to show it was capable of delivering the goods, and fast. Social justice and good governance, fair play and equal opportunity – these are not abstractions that came out of some World Bank manual. They were forged in a Darwinian political struggle between the non-communist left and the pro-communist left. If Mr Lee's chief opponents had been the compradors of the Malayan Chinese Association or the effete conservatives of the Progressive Party, he and his colleagues may not have become the disciplined, focused, determined force that they became.

The second was Singapore's tragic stint in Malaysia. Mr Lee has remarked often that Malaysia's and Indonesia's attitudes towards Singapore were a function of their own domestic racial politics, and that was why Singapore had to have a strong government – to ensure the country was not rolled over. One might wonder if Mr Lee was politic to put things so bluntly, but as a matter of historical fact it is impossible to contradict his statement. If it weren't true, Singapore would still be part of Malaysia. It was forced to be independent precisely because there was no other way to maintain racial and religious harmony. In other words, multiracialism, like good governance, was an existential virtue born of tragic experience. It certainly did not come out of some manual for engineering prosperity.

Thinking of Singapore as a machine might be useful up to a point. Beyond that point it is useless, even dangerous. A machine implies automaticity. It implies something achieved, constructed, accomplished. The moment Singaporeans assume that is all there is to their country – a machine that

*Janadas Devan*

137

requires no more than occasional tinkering – we are finished.

Machines don't make people; people make machines. And when a people forget that, the machines they painstakingly built invariably break down. Mr Lee and his Old Guard colleagues never forgot that. History taught them the foundation of statecraft was not mechanics but soul-craft.

## THE PRIMACY OF VALUES

Why did Singapore succeed when so many other post-colonial states did not? Why – unlike most of their fellow anti-colonial heroes in the liberation movements that swept the Afro-Asian world after World War II – did Mr Lee and his comrades achieve more in the relatively prosaic post-colonial period than they did in the heroic anti-colonial era?

The answer to these questions often takes the form of a litany. Singapore got the fundamentals right: political stability, meritocracy, an incorruptible administration. It instituted the rule of law, ensuring the sanctity of contracts and property rights. It made the right economic choices: welcoming multinationals when the reigning wisdom was import-substitution; hewing to prudent fiscal and monetary policies; choosing to leapfrog the region and hook up with global markets; and so on and so forth – the list is long.

And, of course, every item in it is correct. But it still leaves unanswered a crucial question: How come Singapore made the right choices? After all, it is not as though these choices are lodged in some secret book of state-building recipes. And if there is such a book, why did only a few choose to apply its recipes when most did not?

About 30 years ago, Dr Goh made a remark that I think provides a clue to the thinking of Mr Lee and his colleagues, and their approach to statecraft. Dr Goh was then first deputy prime minister and education minister, and

138

had just introduced "moral education" in Singapore schools. At a private gathering, responding to a discussion of how various and different the moral systems of Singapore's component cultures were, he summed up his moral philosophy thus: "It is simple," he growled. "You do good, you will be rewarded. You do wrong, you will be punished."

Few philosophers will endorse that statement but I'm convinced this simple moral regime explains the choices Mr Lee and his colleagues made in Singapore's formative years. They made the right choices because they, and the people they led, were animated by a set of values that made possible correct political, economic and social choices. Leadership – for there was nothing automatic about translating inherited values into viable state institutions – consisted of insisting on the primacy of those values and refusing to compromise on them.

You do good – don't accept bribes, don't run up huge fiscal debts, don't take the easy way out – and you will be rewarded. You do wrong – compromise on meritocracy, give way to atavistic impulses, promise people freebies – you will be punished. It was a moral regime a child could understand but one only a stout-hearted people could have applied systematically.

Social scientists sum up such values as a country's social capital. Till recently, most of them believed this was unrelated "conceptually" to formal state institutions. They believed, for instance, that Japan's "superior growth performance in its high-growth period was due not to culture (that is, informal norms) but to formal institutions such as industrial policies that in theory could be adopted by anyone", as Francis Fukuyama observes in his *State-Building: Governance and World Order in the 21st Century*. But as Professor Fukuyama goes on to argue, this "is very unlikely to be true":

*Janadas Devan*

139

The institutional quality of economic planning agencies in Japan, Korea and Taiwan did not emerge out of a technocratic how-to manual; it had its roots in a mandarin bureaucratic tradition specific to each country... The view that government office presents an opportunity for predatory rent-seeking is one that could have become widespread (in Japan), but did not.[4]

The same opportunities were present in many other new states and they did become widespread there. In some countries, government served as the locomotive of rapid growth; in others, it became an incubus sucking the lifeblood out of society. Obviously, it is not the formal structure but the informal infrastructure that matters. And obviously it is not government as such but certain kinds of government (or misgovernment) that should be the objects of opprobrium.

140

There are two conjoined principles that Mr Lee and his colleagues adopted early: one, government is absolutely necessary; and two, government can only be as good as the people who run it. On one hand, Mr Lee realised early that there can be no nation-building without state-building. Hence the persistent attention he and his colleagues paid to building up the apparatuses of the state. On the other, Mr Lee realised too that formal state institutions were not in themselves sufficient; that culture and values – the informal infrastructure – animating them were just as important as, if not more than, the formal structures. Hence the persistent attention he and his colleagues paid to the calibre of public officials, the values informing the public services and picking the right people – to contest elections, for political office and for the upper reaches of the civil service. No head of government in the modern era anywhere in the world could have spent as much time poring over résumés and interviewing people for various positions as Mr Lee did.

It is possible for a nation or people to persist despite the absence of an effective state, as happened in the histories of old countries like France or China. The cultural construct "China", for example, exceeds the various iterations of the Chinese state: Tang, Ming, Republic of China, People's Republic. The same cannot be said of the construct "the United States of America", which doesn't exist apart from the state that was inaugurated with the US Constitution in 1789. Nor can it be said of newly created countries where the trajectory is clear: state first, nation next – if the state persists. Realising this, Mr Lee and his colleagues were never tempted to limit the state. Much has been made of their eschewal of big government or the welfare state; but equally significant was their rejection of the neoclassical belief that the power of the state should be restricted so as to ensure individual liberty.

A distinction that Prof Fukuyama makes between the *scope* of state activity and the *strength* or *capacity* of the state is relevant here. The first, "which refers to the different functions and goals taken on by governments", can be curtailed or expanded depending on the ideology of ruling parties – curtailed when right-wing parties win power, expanded when left-wing parties do.[5] The second, which refers to "the ability of states to plan and execute policies and to enforce laws cleanly and transparently", cannot be curtailed without risking disaster.[6] Mr Lee and his colleagues always believed in a strong state and they never shied from expanding its scope. His famous antipathy towards the welfare state should not be mistaken for an adherence to limited government.

Midway through Mr Lee's premiership, from the early 1980s onwards, the dominant trend globally was to limit the state. In politics, centre-right parties gained power in many countries; in academia, neoclassical economics

*Janadas Devan*

141

gained ascendancy. Singapore was not immune to this shift and Mr Lee himself oversaw the introduction of market principles in the provision of public goods, most particularly in health services as well as public housing. But neither the strength nor scope of the state was materially reduced – as became obvious in the two major financial crises of the past 15 years, the 1997–98 Asian financial crisis and the 2008–09 global financial crisis. The Singapore government, using its massive reserves, stepped in aggressively to contain the crises.

There is no science of government, only an art. There is no manual detailing how values – "You do good, you will be rewarded; you do wrong, you will be punished" – can be translated into formal state structures. Only a few good men...

## BEYOND STATECRAFT

September 16, 2013 marked not only Lee Kuan Yew's 90th birthday. It marked also the 50th anniversary of the formation of Malaysia on 16 September 1963. On that day, Sabah, Sarawak and Singapore merged with Malaya to form the Federation of Malaysia. Mr Lee turned 40 that day, as he proclaimed on the steps of City Hall: "Whereas it is the inalienable right of a people to be free of foreign domination, to be independent and to form a government of its own choice ... Singapore [as from today, the 16th day of September, 1963] shall be forever a part of the sovereign democratic and independent state of Malaysia."

It is very difficult to see this straight, but what this means is that 16 September 2013 marks also the 50th anniversary of Singapore's independence – from British colonial rule. August 9, 2015 will mark the 50th anniversary of Singapore's independence – from Malaysia. We celebrated September 16 as our national day on only two occasions: in 1963, when Malaysia was formed, and in 1964. By 1965 this independence day was superseded by another: August 9, which of course comes before September 16, and always has.

It is within this fortuitous triangle formed by Mr Lee's birthday, the 50th anniversary of Malaysia's founding and August 9 that I want to locate what I think is the signal quality of Mr Lee and his generation of leaders. My focus will not be Mr Lee's ideas, but the sentiment – the spirit, emotion, passion that run like a bassline through Mr Lee's public life, and in the absence of which his ideas would have counted for nothing.

Those ideas were important, of course. Singapore did undoubtedly essay a number of unique ideas in development: from the early decision to welcome MNCs while the rest of the developing world kept them at arm's length, to establishing a unique system of tripartitism that built on the German and Japanese models; from CPF to HDB; from GIC to NParks; from the Presidential Council for Minority Rights to the system of Group Representation Constituencies (or GRCs). Some of the ideas were very big indeed: for example, the then remarkable notion that a country's external reserves could be divided into two parts: one, what you needed to maintain the value of your currency; and the other, what you can invest for the long term, a notion that led to the creation of GIC decades before the world had even heard of "sovereign wealth funds". Some of the ideas were seemingly small but had long-lasting consequences: for example, the decision to locate the land authority not in the Ministry of National Development but in the Ministry of Law so as to establish a wall between the land authority and the biggest consumer of land.

The image that occurs to one as we recall what went into creating

*Janadas Devan*

Singapore is not that of the nanny or the housekeeper, let alone the East Asian autocrat of caricature. A more apt image might be that of the constant gardener whose careful husbandry – of resources, talent and values – was devoted persistently to fitting everything to a whole. And the statecraft involved here was more than a question of technique. Nation-building is quite different from assembling a Meccano set or a machine. The gardener cannot be distinguished from the garden. Statecraft, especially at the founding of nations, is indistinguishable from soul-craft.

One can, theoretically, produce a compendious bible on development based on Singapore's experience: How to plan industrial parks? How to house 80 per cent of your population in public housing? How to have people save for their own retirement? How to organise a formidable military force? How to plan a city and make it livable and green? How to make sure businesses, government and trade unions work in unison and not tear up one another? How to combat corruption, maintain law and order, enforce the sanctity of contracts? And so on and so forth.

But would it be possible to build another Singapore elsewhere simply by applying all the "ideas", big and small, that might be contained in such a book? Would Singapore itself have become the Singapore of today if, say, the civil service of that time had possessed this book in 1965, but without the gardeners? What was special about these gardeners? (For there was more than one of them, and Mr Lee was the remarkable leader of an extraordinary team.) What defines the soul that fashioned this unique state?

The answer can be found in the fortuitous triangle formed by Mr Lee, September 16 and August 9.

144

## THE FORTUITOUS TRIANGLE

"History," writes Winston Churchill, "with its flickering lamp stumbles along the trail of the past, trying to reconstruct its scenes, to revive its echoes, and kindle with pale gleams the passion of former days."[7] Most Singaporeans have grown up with the same government almost all our lives. We might be excused if we thought the PAP was always dominant, that Mr Lee was born fully grown and armed, as Athena was from the head of Zeus. But that is not how it happened. It took years for the PAP to establish its dominance; years for the legitimacy of the state to be confirmed as more than a legal entity.

In 1959, the PAP won the elections and formed the government of self-governing Singapore with the support of the Communist Party of Malaya. There is no doubt whatsoever that the mass base then was with the extreme left wing led by Lim Chin Siong. When the inevitable split between the pro-communist and the non-communist left came in 1961, the PAP was left with almost nothing: the party lost almost all its branches, and all but a rump of the unions went over to the Singapore Association of Trade Unions, the labour federation associated with the Barisan Sosialis. The PAP almost lost power altogether, hanging on by just one seat in the Legislative Assembly.

The turn really came in 1965 – 10 July 1965, to be precise. That was the day when the moral-political legitimacy of the nascent state was established. The day when the result of a by-election in Hong Lim, right at the centre of Chinatown, became known.

The PAP had lost the constituency twice in a row before: first in a 1961 by-election that Ong Eng Guan, the former mayor and minister for national development, had forced. Ong received 7,747 votes to the PAP's Jek Yeun Thong's 2,820. The second occasion was in the 1963 general election when Ong received about 5,000 votes and the Barisan Sosialis candidate about

*Janadas Devan*

145

2,300. Together they got 64 per cent of the votes. The PAP candidate, Seah Mui Kok, a trade unionist, received a miserable 33 per cent of the votes.

And barely two years later, in July 1965, just a little less than a month before Separation, in a straight fight between the PAP's Lee Khoon Choy and the Barisan's Ong Chang Sam, the PAP won with 60 per cent of the votes. How come? Because the people understood what was at stake. Relations between the Singapore leadership and the federal government in Kuala Lumpur had broken down. There had been racial riots in Singapore in 1964, and Singapore's leaders – in particular S Rajaratnam and Toh Chin Chye – had organised a Malaysian Solidarity Convention, and had embarked on a campaign for a Malaysian Malaysia throughout the Federation. The PAP had lost badly in the 1964 Malaysian general election, with only Devan Nair winning a seat among the nine seats the PAP had contested in Peninsular Malaysia. But by June 1965 it seemed on the way to establishing itself as a power beyond Singapore with its campaign for a Malaysian Malaysia in both the peninsula as well as in Sabah and Sarawak.

Ong Eng Guan's sudden resignation from the Legislative Assembly in June 1965, Singapore's leaders at that time believed, had probably been engineered by Kuala Lumpur to test the PAP's strength. It had lost twice before in the same constituency. If it lost again, its hold on Singapore would have been doubted and the legitimacy of its Malaysian Malaysia campaign severely damaged. If the PAP had lost in Hong Lim, that would have been used as a pretext to crush the party and forcibly change the leadership in Singapore.

Various leaders in the ruling United Malays National Organisation or UMNO had already openly called for Mr Lee's arrest. Even leaders of UMNO's Chinese partner, the Malaysian Chinese Association, had called for

146

his arrest, with one of them urging the Malaysian Prime Minister Tunku Abdul Rahman to "put Lee Kuan Yew away to sober him up".[8]

Word of all this had reached British Prime Minister Harold Wilson, who reportedly told the Tunku that if his government ordered the arrest and detention of Mr Lee, he (the Tunku) need not attend the next Commonwealth Prime Ministers' Conference. As Wilson was to recall later: if Mr Lee were imprisoned "there would be an accident one morning and it would be written off as suicide. ... Easiest thing in the world to organise."[9]

Singapore's leaders made contingency plans. Mr Lee himself would accept arrest – as the leader of the movement, he had little choice. But others in the leadership would escape elsewhere: to Cambodia, where a Singapore government-in-exile would be established, and to London and elsewhere in the world, from where they would continue agitating for a Malaysian Malaysia. John Drysdale reports in his book *Singapore: Struggle for Success* that "Dr Toh had found a 'jungle green' uniform and was preparing for the day when, rather than be arrested, he would take to the jungle as a guerrilla fighter".

Dr Toh was saved from that fate by the PAP's victory in Hong Lim on July 10. People at the heart of Chinatown had seen Singapore's leaders, in particular Mr Lee, fight back ferociously, refusing to be cowed. Their decision to stand by Mr Lee's leadership sealed Singapore's fate. The Tunku and his senior ministers decided Singapore had to go. Thus August 9.

Ultimately, people follow leaders with fire in their bellies. It wasn't ideas – big or small – that established the legitimacy of the state in the crucible of its founding. What established that legitimacy was the conviction that this government was on their side.

On 27 May 1965, Mr Lee addressed the Malaysian Parliament for the last time when he moved an amendment to the motion to thank the King for his opening address. Everyone from Singapore who was present in the Chamber that day describes the event in almost identical words: you could hear a pin drop. When Mr Lee switched to Malay, you could see UMNO backbenchers sit up and listen, and the front bench sink ever deeper into their seats.

> It is no use threatening us, that they are going to take away our local autonomy in Singapore and so on. It cannot be done unless you are going to use the guns and as I have said, you haven't got enough guns... Let us be frank. We did this calculation carefully and methodically. There is no other way ... The threat is not credible ... [We'll] change this, we'll change that ... you will change nothing ... without the consent of the state government and first you've got to win a democratic election in Singapore and we hold it quite democratically, you know ... We never run away from open confrontation as our friends from Barisan Sosialis can testify. We love it, we relish the prospect of a meeting of minds, a conflict of ideas, not of force.

There you have it: Mr Lee's and his generation's finest hour. What is that singular big idea – the big passion, emotion – behind the big ideas? Simply put: guts, courage. Before you can have ideas for a state, there must be a prior decision: this is who we are, this is what we believe and here is where we will make a stand.

Mr Lee and his Old Guard colleagues exemplified above all the truth that successful statecraft is in essence soul-craft.

148

## Endnotes

1 Henri Ghesquiere, *Singapore's Success: Engineering Economic Growth* (Singapore: Thomson Learning, 2007), p. 6.

2 Ibid., p. 7.

3 Ibid.

4 Francis Fukuyama, *State-Building: Governance and World Order in the 21st Century* (Ithaca: Cornell University Press, 2004), p. 30.

5 Ibid., p. 7.

6 Ibid.

7 *Parliamentary Debates (Hansard)*, House of Commons, Fifth Series, vol. 365, 12 November 1940 (London: His Majesty's Stationery Office, 1950), p. 1617.

8 John Drysdale, *Singapore: Struggle for Success* (Singapore: Times Editions, 1984), p. 386.

9 Ibid., pp. 386–387.

PART
5

# FOREIGN AFFAIRS

## Small State Survival

*Chan Heng Chee*

## Playing Chess

*Bilahari Kausikan*

# SMALL STATE SURVIVAL

———

*Chan Heng Chee*

IN THE ARENA of foreign policy, it is difficult to identify which ideas and principles were formulated by Prime Minister Lee Kuan Yew, which by Deputy Prime Minister Goh Keng Swee and which by Foreign Minister S Rajaratnam. In all likelihood, they talked their ideas through as a group. Yet, there was a distinct way in which Mr Lee would put across his ideas. For instance, he expounded less on non-alignment than Rajaratnam did. In his memoirs *Third World to First*, Mr Lee writes that when he returned from his trip to the United States in 1968, Goh and Rajaratnam told him he sounded too pro-American on the Vietnam War and he may have to tone that message down because of the domestic electorate.[1] Clearly, the first generation team had a good working relationship and they shaped each other's messages and ideas. Nonetheless, in this essay, I will try to outline Lee Kuan Yew's distinct thoughts on foreign policy and how they evolved. I will also discuss Singapore's relationship with the US and how Mr Lee came to view and value the US, and his role in the US-China relationship.

## BROAD PRINCIPLES

Countries and leaders work with strategic perspectives and there are tactical ideas. Some have a poor grasp of strategy and may be caught up with just tactical moves. In the case of Singapore, we are fortunate to have a generation of political leaders – Lee Kuan Yew in particular – whose strategic understanding of the world is unparalleled.

Right from the beginning, Mr Lee has been prepared to go against the dominant view and to speak quite candidly on what he considers essential and good for the region's and Singapore's interests, even though what he has to say might be uncomfortable truths. As he once told an American magazine: "I am not interested in being politically correct. I'm interested in being correct."[2] Singapore's leaders, and Mr Lee in particular, are especially fine-tuned to sense the latest temperature in the region. Mr Lee once told an Australian audience that Singapore was like a canary in a coalmine. What will happen in the world or the region will happen to Singapore first.[3]

I believe Mr Lee's most important contribution to Singapore is to have thought through and implemented a strategy for small state survival. Our leaders felt viscerally the vulnerabilities Singapore faced. In 1965, there were not many small states, much less a city-state that came onto the stage to declare: "We are an independent country." Today in the United Nations, 105 members – or more than half of the 193 member states – are small states defined as a country with less than 10 million population. We have honed the strategy so finely that many small states approach us to ask how we did it. When I was ambassador in Washington, small countries in the Caribbean, Africa and Europe sought to know the key to our success. For instance, the Macedonian ambassador was directed by an undersecretary in the Clinton administration to ask me how Singapore succeeded in attracting so much foreign investment.

So what are Mr Lee's ideas on small state diplomacy that have become the hallmark of Singapore's foreign policy?

The most striking fact is how he saw the inextricable link between domestic policy and foreign policy for our survival as a nation state. In the First Parliament, then Prime Minister Lee could not emphasise enough that his government wanted to establish Singapore as a multiracial, multilingual, multicultural society and nation, where races, languages and religions would be treated equally and no community would be discriminated against. This was to differentiate Singapore from Malaysia and the experience of racial hegemony. Mr Lee pointed to the external relevance of this internal principle, i.e. multiracialism as a protective shield. "We have a vested interest in multiracialism and a secular State," he said, "for the antithesis of multiracialism and the antithesis of secularism holds perils of enormous magnitude, not just for the people living in Southeast Asia, but dangers of involvement by bigger powers who see in such a conflict fertile ground for exploitation of either ideological [or] power interests."[4] I believe he was thinking then of Sukarno's Indonesia, the People's Republic of China, and perhaps even Malaysia.

Mr Lee has always been clear about the sort of foreign policy Singapore must adopt. In October 1966, he advocated that "A foreign policy for Singapore must be one as to encourage first, the major powers in this world to find it, if not in their interests to help us, at least in their interests not to have us go worse".[5] Further, "we must always offer the rest of the world a continuing interest in the type of society we project". And even more importantly, because power decides what happens, it behooves us to "always have overwhelming power on our side".[6] We should seek the maximum number of friends with the maximum capacity to uphold what our friends and ourselves have decided to uphold.

He was firm that we should have no aspirations or ambitions to exercise authority beyond persuasive moral authority. He stated: "It must be our constant endeavour to ensure first, the political climate in which the force which can be lent to us can be exercised".[7] In other words, we should always help create that climate of opinion that is supportive of the presence of external powers in our region.

At the age of 86, he spoke of this again in his April 2009 S Rajaratnam Lecture. Small countries have little power to alter the region; a small country must seek the maximum number of friends, while maintaining its freedom as a sovereign and independent nation. Friendship in international relations is not a function of goodwill or personal affection. He said: "We must make ourselves relevant so that other countries have an interest in our continued survival and prosperity as a sovereign and independent nation."[8] This theme comes up again and again in his speeches.

Singapore has long sought to demonstrate to the world that we are relevant, a society that they would have an interest in. Apart from our geostrategic location, we have projected ourselves as a hub, a global city, a pacesetter, an innovator, and ultimately, as I have been often told in Washington, "the country that has the solutions". Probably no other country has relied as much as Singapore on domestic achievements nor needed it as much to achieve its place in the world. Considering its size, its standing is not bad in the pecking order. We do not have the land mass or population that invites respect. We have relied, as Mr Lee suggested, on becoming that useful country, the country in the region that works, that shining red dot, as a strategy of survival. We make ourselves relevant to others so that it is in their interest to have Singapore around. So the domestic and the international are entwined.

In the early years, our survival was not preordained. The vulnerabilities

*Chan Heng Chee*

155

of size were deeply felt. Mr Lee saw the regional waters as rough, with the big fish eating the small fish. He spoke of the small fish caught between the medium fish and the big fish. In defence strategy, we would turn ourselves into a "poisonous shrimp" killing whoever tried to swallow us.[9] One essential principle Mr Lee impressed on the region and the world is that Singapore, though a small country, cannot be pressured by bigger powers. He demonstrated this when Singapore stuck to its decision to execute two Indonesians despite Indonesia's leaning on us to stay the action. We demonstrated this again by standing up to US pressure in the case of American teenager Michael Fay who was caned for breaking the law in Singapore.

Overcoming size and ensuring that size will not determine our destiny is perhaps one of the most important ideas that Mr Lee implanted in Singaporeans. His political colleagues endorsed this idea. It was Rajaratnam who promoted the idea of Singapore as "a global city".[10] Mr Lee enlarged the international space for Singapore by developing good bilateral relationships with the major powers and strong trade ties globally. It was he who suggested we negotiate free trade agreements to further expand our international economic space.

Our leaders chose to identify with the Non-Aligned Movement, a necessary position in order not to be drawn into the Cold War and into any camp. The majority of the developing countries, of which we were clearly one at that time, belonged to this grouping, and it meant acceptance and recognition as an independent state. Multilateralism is essential for small states and Singapore has been an advocate of international forums and regional groupings. Membership in the UN and in ASEAN was pursued right at the start. Today, the Cold War is over but the Non-Aligned Movement lives

156

on. There are the moderates, of which we are one, and the old style anti-Western countries. Singapore's role is to be a bridge between the two camps.

## SINGAPORE AND THE UNITED STATES

Our membership in the Non-Aligned Movement notwithstanding, the theme that recurred frequently in the early days of Mr Lee's thinking was that "small countries need a big friend".[11] In 1965, our security needs post-independence were immediately met by the continuation of the Five Power Defence Pact which brought Singapore, Malaysia, Britain, Australia and New Zealand into a defence alliance, and in that sense put a halt to the deterioration of relations between Malaysia and Singapore. However, it was clear Britain was withdrawing from the region. It was only a question of when. Mr Lee himself wrote that although he viewed the Americans "with mixed feelings", the US was the only power that could push back communism.[12] But he did not know the Americans. He had studied in Cambridge and knew the British, their culture and their thinking; and he had dealt with British officials.

Mr Lee began working with the Johnson administration. In 1968, between October and December, he took a short sabbatical at Harvard to get to know America and Americans better. He met many top American scholars who knew their country and how their government and power works. Mr Lee considers this time very useful. Of all the people he met, he made a lifelong friend in Henry Kissinger. Dr Kissinger is fond of telling his Lee Kuan Yew story to an American audience. Mr Lee had come to Harvard at the height of the anti-Vietnam protests. At a dinner table in Harvard, surrounded by many anti-war academics, the professors complained and railed against the US government and its Vietnam policy, arguing for a hasty pullout and an end to the war. They thought the leader from Asia would be a kindred spirit. According to Kissinger, Mr Lee looked around him, took things in for a few seconds, and said: "You make me sick." He then went into a long exposition of why the US should stay the course in Vietnam. As you know, decades after the war, Mr Lee told the world that the US presence in Vietnam bought non-communist Southeast Asia time so that we could build our political institutions and develop our economies.

So began his and Singapore's long friendship and relationship with the US. To understand this we must remember Mr Lee is a committed non-communist. He fought a long struggle "riding the communist tiger", initially working with the aboveground pro-communist groups and activists. (These are important and differentiating terms in Singapore's political vocabulary of the 1950s and in our history: communist, pro-communist, communist front and the underground communists.) In the '50s and through the '60s, there were two great political struggles facing Singapore. One was anti-colonialism, the other was the struggle for the political identity of Singapore – communist or non-communist. The US was in Vietnam, the US-Japan Mutual Defence Security Treaty was seen as the stabiliser for security and prosperity in the region. But for Mr Lee, the US role in Asia was not just a military one. The US offered markets, technology and investments to the region that no other power could match. This was essential for the emergence of the four Asian tigers and the ASEAN countries.

Eventually, there was another new wind. In 1987, Mr Lee gave the keynote address at the Commonwealth Heads of Government Meeting (CHOGM) in Canada. It was an interesting time. Mikhail Gorbachev had become the president of the Soviet Union. He launched a programme of *glasnost* ("openness"), *perestroika* ("restructuring") and *demokratzatsiya* ("democratisation"). Mr Lee noted the Soviet Union seemed to have lost its ideological fervour for promoting revolution, focusing instead on restructuring the Soviet economy. In China, Deng Xiaoping had embarked on the modernisation of its economy. At the same time, the US economy was in recession and heavily in debt. As communism receded as a threat, Mr Lee wondered whether the US would focus on promoting democracy, press freedom and human rights. He spoke about the relative decline of American dominance. He pointed out that the US and the Europeans were Christian nations. They have a missionary tradition of going out to save heathens. For decades, they had been spending their surpluses to invest in developing countries. The surpluses were now with the Japanese. He was not so sure what Japan would be like. They were Shinto-Buddhists and did not proselytise.[13] In another speech, he said he was comfortable with the US hegemon. He was not so sure of a Japanese hegemon. In an interview following this line of thinking he said, of Japan joining the UN Peacekeeping force, that it was like "giving liqueur chocolates to an alcoholic".[14] The Japanese go to the limits of whatever they do, whether it is product manufacturing or development; so for Korea, China and Southeast Asia, it was acquiescence, nothing more.

But Mr Lee, like everyone else, did not anticipate the end of the Soviet Union would come so quickly and so decisively and that the world order would be fundamentally changed. The end of the Cold War saw America as the world's hegemon, more powerful than ever before, more confident than before, and triumphalist. During the Clinton administration, America's growth was unparalleled in 30 years, its political position unassailable and Madeleine Albright called her country "the indispensable nation". Europe, mired in its expansion of the European Union (EU), had its own problems.

*Chan Heng Chee*

159

Since then, China's emergence as a major power and the growing economic power of the BRIC nations (Brazil, Russia, India and China) has forced strategic thinkers to come to grips with what all this means for the international system. The US debt and deficit issues have undermined its ambition to remain the world's only superpower for the rest of the century. The US's position was further challenged by the financial crisis of 2008/9 and the ensuing recession. In 2012, China emerged as the No. 2 economy in the world, pushing Japan to third place. Although the US economy is now recovering and China's economy is slowing down, there is no doubt the balance of power is shifting. Mr Lee, in his latest book, *One Man's View of the World*, writes that on the Asian side of the Pacific, "America will over time find it even harder to assert its influence. It will not be business as usual." In this battle of pre-eminence, he sees "Asian nations – lesser powers – will have to adapt accordingly." He admits he feels some "sense of regret at this shifting of power balance because I see America as basically a benign power".[15] It has not been aggressive or acquired territories. When it has fought wars, it has been for a cause.

To him the US-China relationship is the most important relationship of this century. Lee Kuan Yew has made many efforts to help the West understand China; equally, he has sought to explain the United States in all its contradictions to the Chinese. He does not want the two to enter into conflict; he fears they will misunderstand each other, underestimate each other, and miscalculate. His main concern is to ensure a stable US-China relationship, which is the sine qua non for a peaceful and prosperous Asia. Mr Lee sometimes speaks up for one side, and at other times for the other. Singapore's foreign policy is best served by ensuring views going in the wrong direction do not go unchecked. And he sees Singapore's role as being the voice of moderation.

Michael Green, senior director of Asian Affairs in George W Bush's National Security Council, once described Singapore's role as a pilot for the US, guiding the superpower or supertanker into the harbour. Singapore would tell the US, "come in, come in", or at times, "go back, go back", because the US may be overstepping. For example, during the Vietnam War in the late '60s and '70s when voices calling for the United States to bring home the troops and end the war had reached a crescendo, Mr Lee argued for the US to stay. Post-Vietnam, when America could not forget Southeast Asia soon enough and the region grew relatively hostile to the US military presence, Mr Lee spoke of the dangers of US withdrawal from the region. It was in this context that when the US was asked to leave Clark Airbase and Subic Bay, Singapore offered the Americans access to Singapore's military facilities, but not a base.

With the dissolution of the Soviet Union, when the US and Europe, believing the end of history had come, pursued an agenda of promoting democracy and human rights as universal values, Lee Kuan Yew took on the West in a debate on values. Perhaps he saw this as a new form of cultural imperialism. It was in this context that the case of Michael Fay, the American teenager who vandalised more than 20 cars one evening in 1993, became a cause célèbre and precipitated the biggest row in US-Singapore relations. In the West versus East debate, the Western media conveniently ignored the fact that Fay's accomplice was a Hong Kong boy who also received the same sentence of caning. Rather, they seemed more interested in printing the narrative of a Singapore determined to assert Asian values and picking on an American teenager to make a point to the US. After President Clinton's appeal, we reduced the sentence from six strokes of the cane to four. This

*Chan Heng Chee*

161

was not a high point of the bilateral relationship.

Advocated with equal zeal was the "Washington Consensus" that is pushing countries in the region to deregulate their banks, open up their capital accounts, and liberalise trade and accept foreign investment, i.e. to deregulate, deregulate, deregulate. This led to the Asian financial crisis in 1997. Ironically, the crisis singled us out as the one country in ASEAN whose financial system was well managed.

When the US economy began its descent into spiralling deficits and debt, and major Western financial institutions collapsed in 2008–2009, Mr Lee felt compelled to speak out against the "declinist" school – those who argue that America is in decline – because he did not subscribe to it. He remains convinced that the US economy is resilient, has a wealth of creative talent and will continue to do well because it is open to receiving the world's talents.

In the same way, he has spoken up for China. In the 1980s and 1990s, the West dismissed China's growth and its sustainability, some even arguing that the country faced fragmentation. Mr Lee told American and European audiences that China's growth was real and it would be the biggest thing to happen in recent history. He repeatedly told the West that they could not stop China's growth and even if it should stumble for a couple of years, its trajectory was upwards in the long term. He cautioned the US against underestimating China. Today it is the other way round. He has been talking up America much more, explaining why the US will enjoy continued long-term success and remain competitive. He is also concerned that China will underestimate the US.

## PERSONAL RELATIONSHIPS

A discussion of Mr Lee's contributions to the foreign policy of Singapore would be incomplete without highlighting his ability to forge relationships with key world leaders. He puts great store in developing these relationships, which have bought Singapore diplomatic space in international affairs. It is not just a question of bonhomie and sociability (though I have seen Mr Lee charm his hosts in the US). They seek his company for his strategic insights, his understanding of the region and his take on the world. He has a way with words, he puts things succinctly and with the right nuance. He got on particularly well with the Republican presidents Nixon, Reagan and George HW Bush. He is also close to Henry Kissinger, George Shultz and Brent Scowcroft. They are of his generation, and they share the same strategic perspectives.

Mr Lee met President Clinton in 2000. I was then in Washington. Because of the Michael Fay episode, our access to the White House, for a while, was not the same as it had been previously. Then senior minister, Mr Lee was told he would have a meeting with national security adviser Sandy Berger, and President Clinton would do a "drop-by" for about 15–20 minutes. Mr Lee had a conversation with Berger first. Then President Clinton strolled in, Coke can in hand, and sat on the sofa opposite Mr Lee. The room was small, but good for conversation. The back and forth went on and the meeting lasted about 45 minutes. I was told after the meeting that President Clinton was so impressed by Mr Lee that he turned to his officials and demanded, "Why have I not met this man before?"

Later, after he stepped down from the presidency, Bill Clinton came to Singapore a couple of times on his lecture rounds and met with Mr Lee again. He invited Mr Lee to the Clinton Global Initiative (CGI) a few times.

Finally, Mr Lee made an effort to attend a CGI meeting in Hong Kong in December 2008. This was shortly after his heart surgery on 29 November to implant a cardiac pacemaker. He made an effort to show up against his doctor's orders because he had given his word. I am told that as he spoke, the wound on his arm where the drip had been started to bleed, but he kept on speaking. That is the kind of commitment Mr Lee shows. It is not surprising then that he has had good relationships with major captains of industry, the chairmen and CEOs of Fortune 500 companies. They have trusted him, and so they have believed in Singapore.

Mr Lee has received many honours for his achievements. During my term as ambassador, I saw Mr Lee receive four major honours: "The Architect of the Next Century" from the Nixon Center in 1996, the Woodrow Wilson Center Award for Public Service in 2004, the US-ASEAN Business Council's Lifetime Achievement Award in 2009 and the Ford Theatre Trust's Lincoln Medal in 2011. The term "Asian statesman" is frequently used.

Mr Lee's view of himself is quite modest. When asked which statesman in history he would like to have been, he characteristically replied, "I don't want to be remembered as a statesman. First of all, I do not classify myself as a statesman. I put myself down as determined, consistent and persistent. I set out to do something. I keep on chasing it until it succeeds. That is all… Anybody who thinks he is a statesman ought to see a psychiatrist."[16]

Statesman or not, I believe his ideas, speeches and policies on foreign policy will be read and re-read, especially from the perspective of small state survival.

## Endnotes

1 Lee Kuan Yew, *From Third World to First: The Singapore Story 1965–2000* (Singapore: Singapore Press Holdings, 2000), p. 510.

2 "Interview with *Fortune* magazine, 28 May 1997". *The Papers of Lee Kuan Yew: Speeches, Interviews and Dialogues, vol. 12: 1994–1997* (Singapore: Gale Asia, 2013), p. 588.

3 "Question and Answer Session at the Citibank Legacies Dinner, 3 April 2007". *The Papers of Lee Kuan Yew: Speeches, Interviews and Dialogues, vol. 17: 2006–2008* (Singapore: Gale Asia, 2013), p. 239.

4 *Singapore Parliamentary Debates (Hansard)*, 14 December 1965, cols. 114–115.

5 "The Objectives of Singapore's Foreign Policy", speech by Lee Kuan Yew at the University of Singapore Seminar on International Relations, 9 October 1966. *The Papers of Lee Kuan Yew: Speeches, Interviews and Dialogues, vol. 3: 1965–1966* (Singapore: Gale Asia, 2012), p. 526.

6 "The Objectives of Singapore's Foreign Policy", p. 526.

7 Ibid.

8 "The Fundamentals of Singapore's Foreign Policy: Then and Now", speech by Lee Kuan Yew at the S Rajaratnam Lecture, 9 April 2009. *The Papers of Lee Kuan Yew: Speeches, Interviews and Dialogues, vol. 18: 2008–2009* (Singapore: Gale Asia, 2013), p. 400.

9 See, for example, "Big and Small Fishes in Asian Waters", talk by Lee Kuan Yew at the University of Singapore Democratic Socialist Club meeting, 15 June 1966. *The Papers of Lee Kuan Yew: Speeches, Interviews and Dialogues, vol. 3: 1965–1966* (Singapore: Gale Asia, 2012), p. 391.

10 See "Singapore: Global City", talk by S Rajaratnam to the Singapore Press Club, 6 February 1972. Kwa Chong Guan, ed., *S Rajaratnam on Singapore: From Ideas to Reality* (Singapore: World Scientific, 2006), pp. 227–237.

11 "The Objectives of Singapore's Foreign Policy", p. 526.

12 Lee Kuan Yew, *From Third World to First: The Singapore Story 1965–2000* (Singapore: Singapore Press Holdings, 2000), pp. 502–503.

13 "Implications of a World that is Less Bipolar", speech by Lee Kuan Yew at the Commonwealth Heads of Government Meeting, 13 October 1987. *The Papers of Lee Kuan Yew: Speeches, Interviews and Dialogues, vol. 9: 1981–1987* (Singapore: Gale Asia, 2012), p. 712.

14 "Interview with the *International Herald Tribune*, 30 April 1991". *The Papers of Lee Kuan Yew: Speeches, Interviews and Dialogues, vol. 11: 1990–1994* (Singapore: Gale Asia, 2013), p. 88.

15 Lee Kuan Yew, *One Man's View of the World* (Singapore: Straits Times Press, 2013), p. 71.

16 Lee Kuan Yew, *Hard Truths to Keep Singapore Going* (Singapore: Straits Times Press, 2011), p. 370.

# PLAYING CHESS

---

*Bilahari Kausikan*

AN INTERNATIONAL RELATIONS theorist would no doubt call Mr Lee a realist. But no simplistic label can do justice to the eclectic complexity of his approach towards international relations and geopolitics. If any professor of international relations, a field of study to which more than a fair share of nonsense has been attached in the name of theory, were foolhardy enough to ask Mr Lee which of the main schools of international relations – realism, institutionalism, liberalism, constructivism – most influenced him, his reply, if he were in a good mood and if he had even heard of these theories, would probably be "all of the above and none of the above".

## THE PRIMACY OF NATIONAL INTEREST

Mr Lee is an empiricist and a practitioner, not a theorist.[1] He sees the world for what it is and never mistakes his hopes or fears for reality. Mr Lee is not devoid of idealism. After all, he risked his life in the struggle against the communist united front for ideals. Still he knows that in world affairs, as in all fields of human endeavour, not all desirable values are compatible or can be simultaneously realised.

Mr Lee would not, for example, disagree with the proposition that a world governed by international law and international organisations would be preferable for a small country like Singapore. But he would certainly question whether such a state of affairs could be brought about in a world composed of sovereign states of vastly disparate power. He understands that international order is the prerequisite for international law and organisation. So while you may work towards an ideal and must stand firm on basic principles, you settle for what is practical at any point of time, rather than embark on quixotic quests.

And he understands that international law and international organisation are only one among the range of tools available to states, and are not categorical imperatives. In a 1994 interview with *Malaysian Business*, General Tan Sri Hashim "Freddie" Mohammad Ali, former chief of the Malaysian Armed Forces, recalled that Mr Lee had told him that "if PAS (Pan-Malaysian Islamic Party) comes into power ... and tries to meddle with the water in Johor Bahru, I'll move my troops in. I will not wait for the Security Council to solve this little problem."[2]

In so far as any central organising principle guides his strategic thought, it is a laser-like focus on Singapore's national interest. Singapore as we know it today would not exist were it otherwise. He sees the world canvas whole, but unlike too many self-styled "statesmen", Mr Lee has never succumbed to the temptation of capering about on the world stage for its own sake. When he expresses an opinion, it is always to some purpose, even though the purpose may not always be immediately apparent to everyone. He looks at the world strategically with a broad and long-term vision; he plays chess, not draughts.

His strategic and geopolitical thought is infused by an unsentimental view of human nature and power; a view shaped by experience, particularly, as he on several occasions has said, of the Japanese occupation of Singapore.

His analyses are characterised by the hardheaded precision with which he zeroes in on the core of any situation, undistracted by the peripheral. He expresses his ideas directly without cant of any kind.

This is harder to do than you may think and consequently rare. Fluffy thought and weaselly expression are more usual in diplomacy and in the analysis of international relations. For proof of the scarcity of clear thinking on international issues, just peruse the op-ed and international news pages of any major newspaper with an objective eye. And consider, for example, the many knots Western commentators and policymakers have tied themselves into over Iraq, Afghanistan, Egypt, and now Syria. Wishful, ideologically driven thinking, loose talk and the advocacy of impossible or incompatible goals abound.[3]

The disciplined clarity of his thought and expression is one of the primary sources of the influence Mr Lee wields, disproportionate for the leader of a small country like Singapore. His views are valued because they are unvarnished and give a fresh and unique perspective. He says things that leaders of much larger and more powerful countries may well think and may want to say, but for one reason or another cannot themselves prudently say. And so he made Singapore relevant. His support for the Vietnam War at a time when it was politically unpopular around the world – a war he believed unwinnable but nevertheless vital to buy time for non-communist Southeast Asia to put its house in order – is a case in point, as was his support for the US presence in East Asia long before it became fashionable.

Mr Lee has said that he is interested in being correct rather than being politically correct. Margaret Thatcher, the former British prime minister, once said of Mr Lee's analysis, "He was never wrong."[4] Of course, this is not strictly true – Mr Lee has not always been correct. International developments are intrinsically unpredictable and nobody can always be correct. But he has been on target more often than not; and when he has not, he has never been too proud to change his position. So when he speaks, even great powers listen. They may not always like what they hear, but they listen and more importantly, sometimes act on what they hear. In his memoirs Mr Lee has recounted his 1978 meeting with Deng Xiaoping and how he got him to drop Chinese support for communist insurgencies in Southeast Asia. So let me tell you a less well-known story.

In 1981, at the International Conference on Kampuchea held at the UN, the US was poised to sell out Singapore's and ASEAN's interests in favour of China's interest to see a return of the Khmer Rouge regime.[5] The then US assistant secretary of state in charge of China policy attempted to bully and browbeat our foreign minister, saying that there would be "blood on the floor" if we did not relent. We held firm. The assistant secretary then threatened to call Mr Lee personally to complain, thereby exposing his fundamental ignorance of how Mr Lee and the Singapore system operated, despite having previously served as ambassador to Singapore. Our foreign minister calmly and politely invited him to do so. The assistant secretary did not call. The next year Mr Lee travelled to Washington and in a meeting with the Senate Foreign Relations Committee, described America's China policy as "amateurish". Word rapidly spread. As the young desk officer who took notes for that meeting, I was bemused by the spectacle of the assistant secretary frantically scrambling to find out what exactly Mr Lee had said. I don't know if it was coincidental, but the very next year the assistant secretary in question was appointed ambassador to Indonesia – an important position, but one in which he no longer held sway over China policy. And when his new appointment was announced, the gentleman anxiously enquired through an intermediary if Mr Lee had told then President Suharto anything about him. He was reassured and served honourably in Indonesia.

## A PRAGMATIC APPROACH

I do not recount this incident in US-Singapore relations merely for the trite and possibly redundant purpose of illustrating Mr Lee's influence. The moral of the story is his approach to diplomacy, which he hammered into the Ministry of Foreign Affairs but which is not sufficiently understood by the general public and even some sections of our establishment. Diplomacy is not about being nice, polite or agreeable. It is more fundamentally about protecting and promoting the country's interests, preferably by being nice but if necessary by other appropriate means.

In 1968, Mr Lee turned down a direct appeal by then President Suharto to pardon two Indonesian marines who had been sentenced to death for planting a bomb during *Konfrontasi* that killed several Singaporeans.[6] He could not have done otherwise without conceding that the small must always defer to the big and thereby irretrievably compromising our sovereignty. A Jakarta mob then sacked our embassy and threatened to kill our ambassador. But a few years later, in 1973, Mr Lee did not shy away from placing flowers on the graves of the two marines. Both actions – standing firm on fundamental principle even at a risk of conflict and making a gracious gesture once the principle had been established – were equally important in setting the foundations of the relationship we today enjoy with Indonesia. Mr Lee once told an Israeli general who had helped start the Singapore Armed Forces that Singapore had learnt two things from Israel: how to be strong, and how not to use our strength; meaning that it was necessary to get along with neighbours and that no country can live in perpetual conflict with its neighbours.

170

But Mr Lee has had no illusions about the challenges facing a Chinese majority Singapore permanently situated in a Southeast Asia in which the Chinese are typically a less than fully welcome minority. Perhaps his greatest mistake was, during the period when Singapore was part of Malaysia, to underestimate the lengths to which the Malay leadership in Malaysia would go to defend Malay dominance and privileges. This miscalculation led to what was politely termed "Separation" in 1965. But it turned out well for us, better in all probability than if we had remained in Malaysia. At any rate, it was not a mistake that he would ever make again.

The basic issue in Singapore's relations with its neighbours is existential: the implicit challenge a successful Chinese majority Singapore organised on the basis of multiracial meritocracy by its very existence poses to contiguous systems organised on different and irreconcilable principles.[7] This is sometimes dismissed as "historical baggage" that will fade with time. But it is really about the dynamic between two different types of political systems that once shared a common history but have since evolved in very different directions. It is not easy to envisage the fundamental differences ever fading away, even if time blunts their sharpest edges.

Still, even when differences were at their keenest, it did not prevent Mr Lee from working with Malaysia (and Indonesia) based on the pragmatic pursuit of common interests. It is no secret that the relationship between Mr Lee and Dr Mahathir, the former prime minister of Malaysia, was often testy and freighted with history. Less well known is the fact that until the 2010 agreement on railway land, the most significant Singapore-Malaysia agreement since our independence was the 1990 Water Agreement concluded between Dr Mahathir and Mr Lee, then still prime minister. Among other things, it provided for the construction of Linggui Dam.[8]

The incongruity of Singapore in Southeast Asia is the central geopolitical reality from which flowed the constants in Mr Lee's strategic thought and key decisions. These include, among other things, early investment in ASEAN as a stabilising mechanism at a time when it was still uncertain whether ASEAN would survive;[9] his emphasis on the need for a balance of power and the imperative of involving all major powers in regional affairs rather than acquiescing in "regional solutions to regional problems" as our neighbours preferred; the necessity of anchoring the US presence in Southeast Asia, including the offer of the use of our facilities after US forces were no longer welcome in Subic Bay and Clark Airbase in the Philippines; the decision to look forward in relations with Japan and to forgive if not forget, despite his own bitter experiences during the Japanese occupation; a non-ideological approach to working with the former Soviet Union whenever possible despite his anti-communism and staunch opposition to the Soviet invasion of Afghanistan and Soviet support for the Vietnamese invasion and occupation of Cambodia; never giving up on India despite his continuing scepticism about its governance; visiting Vietnam to advise on its economic reforms within months of the 1991 Paris conference that settled post-Vietnamese withdrawal arrangements for Cambodia; and the decision to be the last Southeast Asian country to establish formal diplomatic relations with China despite his early recognition of the inevitable growth of China's influence and the close personal relations he enjoyed with many Chinese leaders.[10]

172

## THE POST-LEE KUAN YEW ERA

No leader, however brilliant, can be internationally influential if he only leads a barren rock. Mr Lee was influential because Singapore is successful. The core operating principles Mr Lee established still form the basis of our foreign policy, although of course their application is continually adjusted to changing circumstances. This should not be surprising since we cannot choose our geopolitical situation and small countries have limited options. But the question inevitably arises: can we continue to be internationally effective and relevant in a post-Lee Kuan Yew era?

Many years ago, the Ministry of Foreign Affairs commissioned a study on how Singapore could continue to have a close relationship with China after Mr Lee's network of personal contacts with Chinese leaders was no longer available. I must emphasise that the study was *not* conducted by a Foreign Service officer because, after lengthy consideration, the conclusion was: have more Lee Kuan Yews!

This was not exactly very helpful. But I am not pessimistic. Mr Lee relinquished executive authority more than 20 years ago; we have in effect already been in a post-Lee Kuan Yew era for quite some time. There will obviously never be another Lee Kuan Yew. But we are still and can remain internationally relevant so long as Singapore is successful and we do not lose the habits of mind – supple, pragmatic, disciplined and unsentimental long-term thinking focused on the national interest – and the core principles and clarity of expression that Mr Lee instilled in what is today a far more institutionalised foreign policy system. So long as we retain this edge, our views will continue to be sought by countries large and small, as indeed they have. Many countries continue to seek to emulate our policies.

But we should certainly not take for granted that we can in fact retain this edge. It is not a God-given right. Domestic politics in Singapore is becoming more complicated. Foreign policy will sooner or later be the subject of domestic debates. This is not necessarily a bad thing, provided – and this is a crucial condition – foreign policy debates occur within nationally agreed parameters of what is and is not possible or desirable for a small country. This is difficult under the best of circumstances and even more difficult for a country with only a very short shared history.

Already and all too often I see the irrelevant or the impossible being held up as worthy of emulation; I see our vulnerabilities being dismissed or downplayed; and I see in civil society and other groups who aspire to prescribe alternate foreign policies only a superficial understanding of how the world really works. Most dangerously of all, I see the first signs, as yet still faint but alas, unmistakable, of failure by some to resist the temptation to use foreign policy as a tool of partisan politics.[11] Whatever the dissatisfaction with the government, however great the desire for change, Singaporeans should not lose sight of the old adage, somewhat clichéd but not invalid: domestic politics should stop at the water's edge. Even the biggest and most powerful countries disregard this adage to their cost and chagrin; for small countries to disregard it could prove fatal. Fortunately, the situation is still reversible.

## Endnotes

1 Mr Lee told a journalist, "I am not great on philosophy and theories. I am interested in them, but my life is not guided by philosophy or theories. I get things done." (Tom Plate, *Conversations with Lee Kuan Yew*, Singapore: Marshall Cavendish, 2010).

2 Shukri Rahman, "An Officer and a Gentleman", *Malaysian Business*, 16 February 1994, pp. 22–24. The threat to our water supply is not just hypothetical but something that has apparently been considered by the Malaysian Armed Forces. In a 2000 article in *Strategi*, an annual publication of the Malaysian Armed Forces College, a certain Lieutenant Colonel Azmy bin Yahya argued that Malaysia had a right to use water as a "strategic weapon" against Singapore, including the possibility to "pollute the supply with either chemical or biological agents" (Lt Col Azmy bin Yahya, "Water as a Factor in International Relations", *Strategi*, November 2000, pp. 14–23).

**3** In a 2008 interview with Arnaud de Borchgrave, Mr Lee quoted with approval the comment by a British official that in Iraq after removing Saddam Hussein, the US should "appoint the strongest pro-Western general and then get out quickly" (Arnaud de Borchgrave, "Interview: Lee Kuan Yew – Part 1", *UPI*, 8 February 2008). Drawing on his experience of the Japanese occupation, in 2003, after the US toppled Saddam Hussein, Mr Lee told Paul Wolfowitz that the Americans had to get the Iraqis to fear them to stabilise the country. The US could not go into Iraq and "become popular by giving out candies and pulling down statues". And referring to what subsequently became of Iraq, Mr Lee said "Democracy, Paul Wolfowitz, mad dog! A country with 4,000 years of history had never anything other than rulers who were autocrats. So that's a total disaster." (Lee Kuan Yew, *Hard Truths to Keep Singapore Going*, Singapore: Straits Times Press, 2011, p. 326).

**4** In her blurb for Mr Lee's memoirs *The Singapore Story*, Margaret Thatcher wrote: "In office, I read and analysed every speech of Harry's. He had a way of penetrating the fog of propaganda and expressing with unique clarity the issues of our times and the way to tackle them. He was never wrong."

**5** With the support of the Soviet Union, Vietnam invaded and occupied Cambodia in December 1978 and installed a puppet government to replace the pro-Chinese Khmer Rouge. Singapore and ASEAN's position was that after the Vietnamese withdrew, there should be UN-supervised free elections to allow the Cambodian people to choose a new government.

**6** *Konfrontasi* was the undeclared war fought between 1963 and 1966 by President Sukarno's Indonesia against the Federation of Malaysia, formed in 1963 by the merger of Malaya, Singapore, Sabah and Sarawak. Singapore was compelled to leave Malaysia in 1965.

176

**7** The special rights and position of the Malays are enshrined in Article 153 of the Malaysian constitution and the organising principle of Malaysian politics is Malay dominance. By contrast, Singapore is organised on the principle of multiracial meritocracy. It was the fundamental and irreconcilable contradiction between Singapore's conception of a "Malaysian Malaysia" in which all races would in principle be equal and the United Malays National Organisation's (UMNO's) insistence on a "Malay Malaysia" based on Malay dominance that made it impossible for Singapore to remain part of Malaysia. In post-Suharto Indonesia, formal legal prohibitions on the use of the Chinese language and celebrating festivals such as the Lunar New Year have been removed, the Chinese are no longer officially classified as "aliens", and pressure on the Chinese to adopt Indonesian names has eased. The current vice-governor of Jakarta is of Chinese origin and there is one Chinese-origin general in the Indonesian armed forces, which would have been unthinkable a few years ago. However, significant informal constraints on the Chinese still remain. Most Chinese in the civil service, police and armed forces are in technical rather than decision-making positions.

**8** Singapore still draws a significant proportion of its water from Malaysia.

**9** The Association of Southeast Asian Nations was formed in 1967 by Indonesia, Malaysia, the Philippines, Thailand and Singapore. Brunei, Vietnam, Laos, Myanmar and Cambodia joined subsequently. ASEAN was preceded by two failed attempts at regional organisation in Southeast Asia – MAPHLINDO (comprising Malaya, the Philippines and Indonesia) and ASA (Association of Southeast Asia) – and there was little reason to believe in 1967 that ASEAN too would not flounder on the same rocks that sank these earlier experiments.

**10** Singapore established formal diplomatic relations with China in October 1990, after Indonesia, which had suspended diplomatic relations with China after a failed 1965 communist coup attempt, normalised relations with it in July 1990. Mr Lee had however visited China on several occasions prior to the establishment of diplomatic relations, starting in 1976.

**11** These signs have been picked up by some sections of the Singapore press. See the commentary in Giam Meng Tuck, "After the Haze", *Lianhe Zaobao*, 13 July 2013. Referring to parliamentary questions by the leader of the opposition Workers' Party, Low Thia Khiang, which had insinuated that the government had turned soft in its dealings with Indonesia on the haze issue, the commentary pointed out, "the haze problem is an environmental issue, but from a broader perspective, it is also a diplomatic issue... Over the years the two senior opposition Members of Parliament, Chiam See Tong and Low Thia Khiang, have been discreet about Singapore's diplomacy with neighbouring countries and knew when not to press the issue to earn political points as it affects Singapore's dealings on the international front. Therefore Low Thia Kiang's questions against the backdrop of increased politicking in Singapore provides food for thought." The commentary concluded, "If the Singapore government's diplomatic stance is deliberately interpreted by the Opposition as 'a sign of weakness', this foreshadows the possibility of foreign policy being drawn into party politics in future. This is a worrying sign." (Unofficial translation from the original Chinese language article.) Another opposition Member of Parliament had earlier drawn attention to Singapore's Middle East policies in an apparent attempt to stir the feelings of Muslim Singaporeans against the government (*Hansard*, vol. 90, Sitting No: 1, Date: 14 January 2013, Section Name: Written Answers to Questions for Oral Answer Not Answered by 3 pm, Question Title: "Abstention From UN Resolution on Palestine". The question was by Pritam Singh.)

# AFTERWORD

▫ *Shashi Jayakumar*

▫ *Rahul Sagar*

# AFTERWORD

---

*Shashi Jayakumar and Rahul Sagar*

IT HAS BECOME FASHIONABLE to ascribe successes and failures in the postcolonial world to a variety of impersonal variables – a country's location, the political institutions and economic foundations established during the colonial period, and the potentially corrupting influence of foreign aid and natural resources. These theories have their merits no doubt, but they underplay the role of leaders – the individuals who, compelled by circumstance and confronted with opportunity, make difficult decisions about how their people should proceed. Our world features many states that once had the advantages of place, history and intellect on their side, and yet today are floundering. In their troubles we see most clearly the value of the leaders who help their fellow citizens steer toward more hospitable waters.

This volume is about one such leader. It is distinctive because for the first time the individuals that worked closely with Mr Lee Kuan Yew have reflected on what they saw and learnt when they worked with him. These essays do not elaborate on Mr Lee's ideas abstractly. Instead they describe the person who framed these ideas and brought them to life, and has defended them tenaciously ever since. If there is a lesson that men and women wishing to be effective leaders can draw from these essays, it is to cultivate a mindset that favours facts over blind faith; that pursues immutable values but never without regard for the consequences; that reflects deeply but is not paralysed by analysis. We are confident that when future generations fully grasp the sum of Mr Lee's achievements and ideas, as reflected in these essays, they will come to understand his dictum that "idealism is the stuff that youthful dreams are made of; experience is the most rigorous tutor of the art of the possible".

This volume emerges out of a conference held in honour of Mr Lee's 90th birthday at the Shangri-La Hotel on 16 September 2013. The conference, hosted by the Lee Kuan Yew School of Public Policy of the National University of Singapore, brought together a stellar cast. We are grateful to the contributors, Dean Kishore Mahbubani, Vice Dean Kanti Bajpai, and to Straits Times Press, for helping us bring these essays to the public in a timely manner. We expect the future to bring more volumes discussing and debating Mr Lee's legacy. We are confident, however, that this collection of essays will always be unique because it is unlikely that so many who know Mr Lee so well, and who are familiar with the workings of his mind, will ever come together and give the measure of Mr Lee in quite the same way.

# THE AUTHORS

## ① *Kishore Mahbubani*

Professor Kishore Mahbubani has had the good fortune of enjoying a career in government and, at the same time, in writing extensively on public issues. He was with the Singapore Foreign Service for 33 years (1971–2004), during which he had postings in Cambodia, Malaysia, Washington DC and New York, where he served two terms as Singapore's ambassador to the United Nations and as president of the UN Security Council in January 2001 and May 2002. He was Permanent Secretary at the Ministry of Foreign Affairs from 1993 to 1998. Currently, he is Dean and Professor at the Lee Kuan Yew School of Public Policy of the National University of Singapore. In the world of ideas he has spoken and published globally. His latest book is *The Great Convergence: Asia, the West, and the Logic of One World.*

## ② *SR Nathan*

SR Nathan is one of Singapore's most distinguished public servants. Born into poverty, he survived family tragedy, destitution and the Japanese occupation. After getting a university diploma as an adult, he worked his way through the civil service ranks to become successively a mediator in trade union disputes, a foreign affairs expert, Chairman of Straits Times Press, a diplomat and a two-term President of Singapore.

He has been an eyewitness to Singapore's history before and after independence, with an insider's view of many key events at home and abroad.

### ③ Heng Swee Keat

Heng Swee Keat was elected a Member of Parliament for Tampines GRC on 7 May 2011. He was appointed Minister for Education on 21 May 2011. Prior to this, he was the Managing Director of the Monetary Authority of Singapore. He has also served as the Permanent Secretary of the Ministry of Trade and Industry, overseeing economic policy, trade negotiations, and the regulation and development of industry. Before assuming this appointment, he was the Chief Executive of the Trade Development Board. He has also served in various other positions in the Singapore Civil Service.

Between 1997 and 2000, Heng Swee Keat served in the Prime Minister's Office as the Principal Private Secretary to then-Senior Minister Lee Kuan Yew. In 2001, he was awarded the Gold Medal in Public Administration; in 2010, he received the Meritorious Medal for his contribution to the Public Service in Singapore.

### ④ Chan Sek Keong

Born on 5 November 1937 in Ipoh, Perak, Malaysia, Chan Sek Keong graduated from the University of Malaya in Singapore with a Bachelor of Laws (Hons) degree in 1961. He was called to the Malayan Bar and the Singapore Bar a year later.

He practised as a lawyer in the Federation of Malaya and Singapore for 24 years before joining public service in Singapore for 26 years as a judicial commissioner/judge of the Supreme Court of Singapore, Attorney-General and finally as Chief Justice of Singapore. He retired on 5 November 2012.

As Attorney-General, he advised the government on many public law issues and delivered many judgments on such issues as judge. He has also given many lectures and speeches and has published papers on public law and on the rule of law in Singapore.

## ⑤ S Jayakumar

Professor S Jayakumar was former Deputy Prime Minister (2004–2009) and Senior Minister (2009–2011). He joined politics in 1980 and held various portfolios such as Minister for Home Affairs, Minister for Foreign Affairs, Minister for Labour, Minister for Law, and Co-ordinating Minister for National Security. He oversaw the Pedra Branca case before the International Court of Justice as well as the Singapore-Malaysia land reclamation case before the International Tribunal for the Law of the Sea. Professor S Jayakumar has written several books, the most recent being *Pedra Branca – The Road to the World Court* with Professor Tommy Koh and *Diplomacy – A Singapore Experience*.

Prior to entering politics, he served as Dean of the Faculty of Law at the National University of Singapore. After retiring from politics in 2011, he returned to the University. He is also consultant at the law firm Drew and Napier.

## ⑥ Peter Ho

Peter Ho is the Senior Adviser to the Centre for Strategic Futures and a Senior Fellow at the Civil Service College. He is also Chairman of the Urban Redevelopment Authority of Singapore and of the Singapore Centre on Environmental Life Sciences Engineering.

When he retired from the Singapore Administrative Service in 2010 after a career in public service stretching more than 34 years, he was Head of the Civil Service, concurrent with his other appointments of Permanent Secretary (Foreign Affairs), Permanent Secretary (National Security and Intelligence Coordination) and Permanent Secretary (Special Duties) in the Prime Minister's Office. Before that, he was Permanent Secretary (Defence).

## ⑦ Yong Ying-I

Yong Ying-I is a career public servant who has served in various agencies including the Ministries of Finance, Trade & Industry, Home Affairs, Communications & IT, Manpower and Health, the last two of which as their Permanent Secretary. An economist and MBA by training, she was the founding CEO of the Infocomm Development Authority (IDA), the founding Chairman of the Workforce Development Agency, and served as Principal Private Secretary to then-Deputy Prime Minister Lee Hsien Loong.

She presently helms the Public Service Division of the Prime Minister's Office as the Singapore Government's chief human resource officer, with the goal of sustaining a first-class Public Service. She also guides the Public Service to be future-ready, to be better prepared for longer-term challenges and risks. She leads the National Research Foundation, which is the Prime

Minister's programme office guiding the nation's research, innovation and enterprise strategies, funding research programmes nation-wide and catalysing new capability development. She is Chairman of the Civil Service College as well as Chairman of IDA. She also serves on the Boards of the Singapore China Foundation and the Singapore Symphony Orchestra.

## ⑧ *Seng Han Thong*

A journalist for 21 years with the Chinese press of Singapore Press Holdings, Seng Han Thong entered Parliament in 1997. He is currently Deputy Chairman of the Government Parliamentary Committee (GPC) for Transport, member of the GPC for Manpower and member of the Government Cut Waste Panel. He is also the Chairman of Singapore Taxi Academy, a board member of Singapore Chinese Orchestra and a member of Ngee Ann Kongsi Committee of Management.

Over the years, Seng has sat on various government statutory boards, including Public Utilities Board, Land Transport Authority, Information Development Authority, Civil Aviation Authority of Singapore, Ngee Ann Polytechnic and Nanyang Polytechnic.

He was also Assistant Secretary-General of the National Trades Union Congress from 1999 to 2012 and CEO of NTUC Media Co-operative from 2006 to 2011. He has been adviser to a number of trade unions and Chinese clans, as well as cultural and trade associations.

## 9 Janadas Devan

Janadas Devan, Director of the Institute of Policy Studies, was educated at the National University of Singapore and Cornell University in the United States. He taught English in various institutions in Singapore and the US, and later wrote for a range of publications in the region, before joining *The Straits Times* in 1997.

He served as the paper's leader writer for many years, writing unsigned editorials on a wide variety of subjects. He wrote a weekly column on politics and economics, in which he covered international and domestic developments. He also wrote a column on language for *The Sunday Times*. In 2008, he became the editor of the paper's opinion pages, and in 2010, became the paper's associate editor. He also did a weekly radio broadcast, "Call from America", for Radio Singapore International, from 2000 to 2008, on American life and society.

He left *The Straits Times* in July 2012 on being appointed the government's Chief of Communications at the Ministry of Communications and Information.

## 10 Chan Heng Chee

Chan Heng Chee is ambassador-at-large with the Singapore Ministry of Foreign Affairs and Chairman of the Lee Kuan Yew Centre for Innovative Cities in the Singapore University of Technology and Design. She is also Chairman of the National Arts Council. In July 2012, she was appointed a member of the Presidential Council for Minority Rights, and in November 2012, as Singapore's representative to the ASEAN Intergovernmental Commission on Human Rights.

Ambassador Chan has served as Singapore's ambassador to the United States, Singapore's permanent representative to the United Nations, high commissioner to Canada and ambassador to Mexico. Previously, she was Executive Director of the Singapore International Foundation and Director of the Institute of Southeast Asian Studies. She was the founding Director of the Institute of Policy Studies.

## *11* *Bilahari Kausikan*

Bilahari Kausikan is currently ambassador-at-large at the Ministry of Foreign Affairs (MFA). Prior to this he was the Permanent Secretary of MFA from 2010 to 2013, and Second Permanent Secretary from 2001. He has also held other positions in the ministry and abroad, including as Singapore's permanent representative to the United Nations in New York and ambassador to the Russian Federation.

# INDEX

190

191

195